Writing the Icon of
THE HEART

Also by Maggie Ross
The Fire of Your Life: A Solitude Shared
The Fountain and the Furnace: The Way of Tears and Fire
Pillars of Flame: Power, Priesthood and Spiritual Maturity
Seasons of Death and Life: A Wilderness Memoir

Text copyright © Maggie Ross 2011
The author asserts the moral right
to be identified as the author of this work

Published by
The Bible Reading Fellowship
15 The Chambers, Vineyard
Abingdon OX14 3FE
United Kingdom
Tel: +44 (0)1865 319700
Email: enquiries@brf.org.uk
Website: www.brf.org.uk
BRF is a Registered Charity

ISBN 978 1 84101 878 2
First published 2011
10 9 8 7 6 5 4 3 2 1 0

Acknowledgments
Unless otherwise stated, scripture quotations are taken from the New Revised Standard
Version of the Bible, Anglicised Edition, copyright © 1989, 1995 by the Division of Christian
Education of the National Council of the Churches of Christ in the United States of America,
and are used by permission. All rights reserved.

Quotations from the Psalms in the essay 'Cranberries' are taken from the 1979 BCP Psalter,
and verse references follow the numbering in that version.

'But the silence in the mind…' by R.S. Thomas, *Collected Later Poems: 1988–2000* (Bloodaxe
Books, 2004). Reprinted by permission of Bloodaxe Books.

A catalogue record for this book is available from the British Library

Printed in Singapore by Craft Print International Ltd

Writing the Icon of
THE HEART

IN SILENCE BEHOLDING

MAGGIE ROSS

For
Marion Glasscoe
Scholar, Mentor, Friend

ACKNOWLEDGMENTS

The essays in this book have been revised and rewritten. In their original form they were published in the following journals. 'Cranberries', 'Whatever Happened to Discretion?', 'The Space of Prayer', 'The Walrus of the Living God', 'Writing the Icon of the Heart', 'Remembering to Forget', 'Barking at Angels', 'Liturgy in Truth' and 'Practical Adoration' were all published in *Weavings* between 2003 and 2008. 'Tears and Fire' was first published in *Sobornost* (Spring, 1987). 'The Ecology of Repentance' was published in the now defunct magazine *Creation* in September, 1992. 'Heaven Can't Wait' appeared in *Heaven* (ed. Roger Ferlo, Seabury Press, 2007).

Many people provided personal support and encouragement during the revision of these articles; there is room to mention only a few. Naomi Starkey has offered patient editorial advice and information. Professors Sebastian Brock, Vincent Gillespie and John Barton, all of Oxford University, have been faithful friends, colleagues and mentors for more than two decades. There are no words to describe what Marion Glasscoe has taught me. John Mogabgab and Pamela Hawkins gave incisive editing for the earlier versions of the essays published in *Weavings*. The late Abbot Conway, along with Rachael Mitchinson, Beth Edwards and Frazer Crocker, have made always helpful comments and suggestions. Special thanks to Terri Hobart for incomparable line editing, to Lucy who provided comfort during this challenging process, and to Mike, Tate and Jack for Texas hospitality. My gratitude also to Bill Countryman and John Coolidge, who have been helping me with Greek and Hebrew; any mistakes are entirely mine. I am also grateful for the always unfailingly courteous and friendly assistance of the staff of Duke Humfrey's library at the Bodleian. The All Saints Sisters of the Poor in Oxford provided housing over a number of winters for a peppercorn rent. And last but certainly not least, my thanks to John and Margie Thelen, who provide a port in a storm.

But the silence in the mind
is when we live best, within
listening distance of the silence
we call God. This is the deep
calling to deep of the psalm-
writer, the bottomless ocean
we launch the armada of
our thoughts on, never arriving.

It is presence, then,
whose margins are our margins;
that calls us out over our
own fathoms. What to do
but draw a little nearer to
such ubiquity by remaining still?

R.S. THOMAS

CONTENTS

The essays are best read in the order in which they appear.

✳

FOREWORD

'I had it on the tip of my tongue.' Everyone has had the experience of not quite remembering a name or a word, and the experience gets more common with age. The word we are looking for lies just out of range, and, as we turn our inward eye to see it, it slips further away. The more intently we think about it, the more it evades our grasp. The only solution is to stop paying it conscious attention; then it suddenly pops into our mind unbidden, just before sleep or when we are thinking (or think we are thinking) about something else.

This phenomenon is sometimes called the paradox of intention, and it points to two different ways of 'paying attention'. One involves straining every nerve to concentrate on something, which we then fail to find. The other is a matter of having a habit of being aware of things that are not ourselves, in a way that allows what we know to surface in our mind. This second kind of attention cannot be deliberately practised, but depends on our whole mental state. It is something like what Maggie Ross calls 'beholding': holding ourselves open for reality to impinge on us. In a world of distraction and striving, it is the special kind of passivity in the face of reality that we most need.

This is not a book about 'spirituality'—acquiring spiritual 'experiences'—but about being open to reality, which includes and indeed is rooted in the reality of God. 'Beholding is organic, ungrasping and self-emptying' (p. 12). This book is intended for everyone who has had enough of 'spiritual writing' and is looking for something that will make sense of normal human experience and integrate it into the knowledge of God through Christ.

John Barton
Oriel & Laing Professor of the Interpretation of Holy Scripture,
University of Oxford

INTRODUCTION

How long shall I be in the world of the voice and not in the world of the word? For everything that is seen is voice and is spoken with the voice, but in the invisible world there is no voice, for not even voice can utter its mystery. How long shall I be voice and not silence, when shall I depart from the voice, no longer remaining in things which the voice proclaims? When shall I become word in an awareness of hidden things, when shall I be raised up to silence, to something which neither voice nor word can bring. [1]

There is a silence of the tongue, there is a silence of the whole body, there is the silence of the soul, there is the silence of the mind, and there is the silence of the spirit... The silence of the spirit is when the mind ceases even from stirrings caused by spiritual beings, and when all its movements are stirred solely by Being; in this state it is truly silent, aware that the silence which is upon it is itself silent. [2]

Silence is context and end, beholding the means. In the final analysis, this is all we need to know.

This silence is not the absence of noise; it is the vast interior

9

landscape that invites us to stillness. At its heart, in our heart, it is the Other. Silence is not in itself religious, but to express the ineffable joys found in its depths is almost impossible without metaphors that frequently sound religious.

Silence and beholding coinhere, mutually informing one another.

Beholding, also, is not in itself religious; the primordial silence we engage in beholding is unnamable and not an object. Beholding leaves traces in its context and bestows an energy that is likewise often expressed in religious metaphor.

If the silence and the beholding that underlie these metaphors are not acknowledged and understood, we cannot interpret any of the texts that refer to the processes of the interior life, including Scripture. For example, in the Bible the imperative form of the word 'behold' has more than 1300 occurrences in Hebrew and Greek. After God has blessed the newly created humans, the first word he speaks to them directly is 'Behold' (Genesis 1:29). This is the first covenant, and the only one necessary; the later covenants are concessions to those who will not behold. In the NRSV the word 'behold' appears only 27 times in the Old Testament and the Apocrypha, and not at all in the New Testament.

Without the 'behold', how are we to understand the end of Matthew's Gospel, 'Behold! I am with you always, to the end of the age' (28:20)? For it is in the covenant of beholding that the risen Christ is with us until the end of time. The movement of beholding is a lived recapitulation of the en-Christing of Philippians 2:5–11. The word the NRSV uses in Matthew 28:20 instead of 'behold'— 'remember'—has nothing of this covenant of engagement or self-emptying. It debases the text and raises the question, 'How is the risen Christ with us until the end of time?' Does he flit about like Caspar the ghost, saying, 'Catch me if you can'? The word 'remember', among other faults, is one-sided and dualistic. It seeks to circumscribe and control. It struggles unsuccessfully to express what is implicit in the word 'behold'. The NRSV has taken a restatement of the first covenant of Genesis and turned it into an isolated memory that reduces those whom Jesus leaves behind to orphans, abandoned and alienated.

Hebrew and Greek authors are careful to distinguish bodily seeing from beholding or inward vision. Jesus himself comments on the use of the word 'behold' in Luke 17:21 (echoed in Matthew 24:26 and Mark 13:21). Having lost the sense of 'behold', most modern translators make a hash of this passage. The New Jerusalem translation is arguably the worst, missing entirely the internal clue as to whether *entos* should be translated 'within' or 'among'. In the context of what was said above about beholding, the passage may be interpreted as follows. The kingdom of heaven is not an observable phenomenon of which you might say, 'Look, here it is' or 'Look, there it is', using the analytical observation of the bodily eye. Neither 'behold' nor the kingdom of heaven is subject to linear, worldly analysis. Even if someone says, 'Behold, here it is' or 'Behold, there it is', don't believe him; it's a misuse of the word 'behold'. The word 'behold' is appropriate only to the invisible kingdom of heaven within you, and that kingdom *is* beholding.[3] By extension, the kingdom of heaven cannot be manifest *among* you until it is manifest *within* you. Beholding entails all the moral and ethical outward behaviour that Jesus teaches. To put this more simply, ordinary seeing is analytical; it discriminates, grasps and controls. Beholding is organic, un-grasping and self-emptying.

Silence and beholding are our natural state. As Irenaeus puts it, 'The glory of God is the human being fully alive, and the glory of the human being is the beholding of God': the two clauses are interdependent.[4] The story of the garden of Eden tells us of the primordial distraction from beholding, the descent into noise and the bewilderment caused by the projections we call 'experience'. All our ills come from the loss of silence and beholding, our failure to listen and our insistence on our flawed and limited interpretations. In was in the context of beholding that we were given stewardship of the earth; it is in the context of distraction

11

that we have (mis)managed it. As the pace of contemporary life accelerates and the rising tide of noise degrades the biosphere, the need to recover and, more especially, to practise silence and seek into the beholding becomes ever more critical. This is especially true for institutional religion.

One of the reasons for writing this book is to attempt to make more accessible the assumptions about silence and beholding that underlie the often arcane language of the interior life. To do this, I have often referred to key functions of the brain that are familiar to everyone. The paradox of intention is the one most critical to both silence and the religious metaphors that refer to it, and it turns up in these essays in a number of guises. I have illustrated some of these observations about the mind with quotations from Isaac of Nineveh, whose unsurpassed writing on the spiritual life is underpinned with a psychological acuity that was widespread among ancient and medieval writers. In many ways they knew more about the way the mind works than we do; some of the most basic insights—such as how we arrive at insight—have corollaries in recent neurobiological studies. This correlation does not 'prove' anything, however; it rather shows convergence at a cellular level with what had been common knowledge for millennia until about the middle of the 15th century, when the practice of silence was suppressed by the Western church.

As this is a book of essays (a more comprehensive and systematic study is forthcoming), the central themes are prismatic, refracting throughout the book. Thus it might be useful to list some of the themes in orderly fashion.

- We need to recover the lost word 'behold', to restore it to its central place in the Judeo-Christian textual tradition and to theology and practice.

- Silence is not an absence of noise (though that sort of silence helps) but a limitless interior space.

- Silence is our natural state. Lack of silence erodes our humanity.

- Silence is religiously neutral; it is the interpretation of what happens in the silence that tends to give rise to religious metaphor and doctrine. The debate over whether or not religion is innate to human beings has so far overlooked this consideration. It has also ignored the centrality of paradox, which links the superficial conceptual linear brain to the deep inclusive global brain where connections are made and from which insights arise, over which we have no control but which we can put to use through intention.

- In speaking of the work of silence, the word 'mind' refers to the whole person, not a disembodied energy (which, in this life, anyway, is an impossibility). The work of silence can be done entirely outside religion, though religious metaphors rightly used have the capacity to enlarge interior boundaries. Silence must be fed.

- Through intention we can teach our selves to default to silence; meditation is only a first and very minor step.

Finally, a word about words. The word 'mystic' appears in this book only three times—twice in quotations, and once as a negative. It is a word that has, in my view, become entirely useless. It has acquired nuances of romanticism, exoticism and self-absorption. In addition, far too many studies of 'mysticism' and 'spirituality' are based on a modern and narcissistic notion of 'experience' as self-authenticating that corresponds neither to the way the brain works nor to notions of experience in the ancient and medieval worlds, which in fact do correspond to the way the brain works.

The words 'transcend' and 'transform' also do not appear in this book except in quotations. Both words are disincarnating. The interior life leaves nothing behind ('transcend'), nor is one thing changed into another ('transform'). There is no magic involved; frogs do not change into princes or princesses. The use of both of these words has done incalculable harm to the interpretation and transmission of what is meant by 'spiritual maturity'.

Instead, through beholding we are transfigured in every sense: nothing is wasted, nothing is left behind; through our wounds we are healed; our perspective—the way we 'figure things out'— is changed. In the resurrection, the wounds of Christ do not disappear; they are glorified. Only the devil appearing as Christ has no wounds, being too vain to bear them.

To summarise: in our core silence, through our beholding, we realise our shared nature with God; we participate in the divine outpouring upon the world: incarnation, transfiguration and resurrection become conflated into a single movement of love.

Feast of Julian of Norwich, 8 May 2010

CRANBERRIES[5]

Moses did not know that the skin of his face shone because he had been talking with God.
EXODUS 34:29

September in the heart of Denali, just outside the border of the national park near the old mining town of Kantishna: the silent land is expectant. The first blanket of snow could come at any time. The tundra is suffused with the slanting light of a lingering sun; the heavy golden air is filigreed with the hoarse fluting of cranes as they spiral to the heavens. The Mountain's [6] presence is tactile. Wickersham Wall, the 15,000-foot expanse of sheer grey granite, seems close enough to touch, though it is 30 miles away as the raven flies, across a landscape saturated with autumn, soaked with the radiance of cranberries.

Cranberries: low-bush cranberries, to be specific. Easily overlooked, trodden underfoot, they spring back from their bed of Labrador tea, unbruised and unhurt. Growing with blueberries and crowberries, they provide some of the loveliest patterns of colour in nature. When half-ripe they are brilliant scarlet against the blue-silver of new spruce growth, the russet of bearberry or the grey of reindeer lichen; their brilliant hues hint of Christmas. As the cranberries ripen, their scarlet transmutes into a darker purple-red;

they become harder to find. Once made brilliant by bright sun, their subdued maturity is now made visible in the more subtle light of high clouds or the sheen of mist and rain.

Cranberries. I've been living with cranberries for a week now, gallons of them. To be out in the vastness amid their prodigal abundance makes me glad I have to pick them on my knees. I go out with my backpack, some gallon jugs and the berry rake. When I find patches where berries grow thick enough to use it, I feel rather like a small bear, clawing with my wooden paw through the vegetation, putting the harvest into containers instead of my mouth. Slowly the jars fill, and slowly my backpack becomes heavier.

Late one sunny afternoon I brought my haul back to camp, rolling the cranberries by handfuls down an inclined frame on which a piece of woollen blanket had been stretched, the rough cloth catching the bits of leaf and moss that inevitably are picked with the berries. They rattled on to a flat tray, the crimson punctuated by the odd blueberry or crowberry.

When the tray was full, I looked at it as if for the first time and caught my breath. A phrase from Psalm 34 leapt to mind, 'Look on me and be radiant...' (v. 5). I picked up the tray of radiance and set it on the bench outside the food storage cache where the angled light made the berries glow ever more deeply from within.

This same radiance extends to everyone at our camp, guest or staff, no matter what the weather; it shines from their faces. They arrive tired and stressed, travel-weary, even a little suspicious if they are first-timers, not knowing quite what they will find in the people or the wilderness. But soon the quiet magic of the land takes hold: a caribou against the horizon; a bear cavorting among the willow; a wolf at its kill; tiny spring flowers still to be found among the few snow patches remaining from last winter; a pair of ravens soaring overhead, calling, calling; the cloudy drape drawing back from The Mountain to reveal its glory.

This glory of cranberries and wilderness bestows humility in the radiance that captures us and is reflected in our faces. It is most present when we are least self-conscious, when our awareness is focused outside ourselves and we are briefly taken into a space where the ordinary preoccupations of time are laid aside. Above all, it is a gift, as the cranberries themselves are a gift. This radiance is the trace of divine love that creates and sustains, lingering in all creation, no matter how muted it may seem. The ability to see this love depends on our receptivity to the gift of humility, which is contemplation, purity of heart and peace all rolled into one, the single virtue of which the paradoxes of the Beatitudes speak.

Put more simply, only love can recognise Love. It is only because we bear, each one of us, each fragment of creation, the trace of the divine that we dimly recognise that the hunger crying out from every human heart can be fed by this radiance alone.

It is these commonplace cranberry events that underlie the wisdom of the Judeo-Christian heritage. The psalms are full of such references. God needs mere fingers to make the heavens, the stars and the moon (Psalm 8:4); he sports with Leviathan (104:28) and feeds the young ravens when they cry (147:10). The psalms refer not only to the natural world but also to the profound effect that world has on us, what it reveals of our psychology and character. The phrase from Psalm 34 is an example: look on me and be radiant, and let not your faces be ashamed (v. 5).

For in the light of this radiance, all else is forgotten, all that preoccupies and troubles us, all our pain and dismay. It is not that they are excised or erased but, as the contemporary philosopher Erazim Kohàk has remarked, our pain becomes part of something larger than ourselves, and is transfigured. In his book *An Evil Cradling*, a modern *Dark Night of the Soul*, Brian Keenan describes the moment when, in the midst of despair induced by solitary confinement, he was given an orange. Starved as he was for fresh fruit, he could not bear to eat it but could only behold the wonder of its colour, its form, its radiance in the dark.

Through these transfigurations, we realise concretely what the ancients knew—our participation in the divine nature. We are with Moses and the elders, whose beholding on the mountain and its effects constitutes one of the biblical passages most frequently cited by contemplative writers. This same beholding is promised to all of us, as summed up in the sublime vision of Revelation:

Then the angel showed me the river of the water of life, bright as crystal, flowing from the throne of God and of the Lamb through the middle of the street of the city. On either side of the river is the tree of life with its twelve kinds of fruit, producing its fruit each month; and the leaves of the tree are for the healing of the nations. Nothing accursed will be found there any more. But the throne of God and of the Lamb will be in it, and his servants will worship him; they will see his face, and his name will be on their foreheads. And there will be no more night; they need no light of lamp or sun, for the Lord God will be their light, and they will reign for ever and ever. (Revelation 22:1–5)

Our seeking into the beholding is not a matter of rejecting the particularities of creation but rather plunging into their deepest heart, allowing them wholly to draw our attention. 'Amor meus, pondus meum,' said St Augustine. Love draws everything to itself, and this radiant love is the source of all fruitfulness.[7]

BARKING AT ANGELS

In the bleak mid-winter
Frosty wind made moan,
Earth stood hard as iron,
Water like a stone.
Snow had fallen, snow on snow,
Snow on snow,
In the bleak mid-winter
Long ago.

A few years ago, the Bodleian Library published a Christmas card that showed the annunciation to the shepherds—or, rather, to one shepherd, standing on a hillside shielding his eyes from the glory of the herald angel. Beside him, his cheeky dog is doing what good sheepdogs do: barking at the strange intruder. It is not hard to imagine the poor shepherd, in dread and awe of this staggering vision, trying to get the dog to shut up long enough for him to hear what the angelic messenger is saying.

I often wonder if all the fretful, frenetic activity in our lives isn't a human way of barking at angels, of driving away the signs that are everywhere around us; signs that are calling us to stop, to wake up, to receive a new and larger perspective, to pay attention to what is most important in life, to behold the face of God in every ordinary moment. These signs press on us most insistently at the turning of the year, when earthly light drains from our lives and we are left wondering in the dark.

The church, from ancient times, recognised the spiritual value of this winter span of darkness and created in its liturgy what we might think of as a three-months-long Night Office, beginning with the Feast of All Saints on 1 November and ending with Candlemas on 2 February. This season is a vast parabola of prophecy and vision, a liturgical arcing of eternity through the world's midnight.

The readings—especially those from Isaiah and Revelation—do their best to subvert our perceptions of time and space in order to plunge us into the great stillness at the heart of things, the stillness necessary to make space for what is 'ever ancient and ever new'[8] to break through the clamour of our minds, to open our hearts to the Beloved, to annunciation and to fruition. Eternity is our dwelling place even in time, if only we have the eyes to see, the ears to hear, the heart to welcome. 'Holy, holy, holy is the Lord of hosts,' cry the seraphs, their voices shaking the foundations even as their ineffable wings fold us into the stillness of God (Isaiah 6:3).

Only in this stillness can we know that eyes are being opened and ears unstopped; that the lame are leaping like deer and those once silenced singing for joy; that water is springing in the parched wilderness of our pain. Only as we are plunged into the depths of this obscure stillness can we know the wonderful and terrible openings of the seals and the book; the rain of the Just One; the heavens rent by angels ascending and descending; the opening of graves and gifts, of hell and the side of Christ.

✳

Our God, heav'n cannot hold Him,
Nor earth sustain;
Heav'n and earth shall flee away
When he comes to reign.
In the bleak mid-winter
A stable-place sufficed
The Lord God Almighty,
Jesus Christ.

By contrast, it is a curiously contemporary phenomenon that the public rhetoric of religion employs words such as 'freedom' and 'liberty' even while it is taking away our sense of wonder, crowding our minds with insistent demands and obviating the possibility of any space for contemplation. Thus we are invited to think about our selves and our discontents, especially our fear, which locks us in time instead of gesturing towards eternity.

By associating God with fear, political and religious institutions encourage us to calibrate certainty by establishing rigid conceptual grids. We then try to force our selves and our world to conform to these templates, an exercise that ends in an illusory sense of control. This tragic search for security in exterior validation makes us hostage to what other people think, especially the opinions of those who seek to define the boundaries and content of our lives. Our anxiety is so great that even the fickle wind of chance cannot break our death-grip on the wildly vacillating weathervane of others' opinions. This desperate clinging to convention can extend to being afraid to talk about God—or even to pray—out-side carefully scripted parameters, in spite of the fact that such denatured language can twist the thoughts, words and intentions of our hearts.

True Christianity stands in opposition to such closed systems. Its essential message is this: to 'free those who all their lives were held in slavery by the fear of death' (Hebrews 2:15). The fear of death can take many forms, most of which have little to do with what might happen after our bodies die. Rather, fear of death is a matter of the mind. It has everything to do with how we perceive and interpret our experience. Our self-consciousness generates anxieties that make us vulnerable to manipulation and coercion in every sphere of our lives, from the most trivial preoccupation with fashion to the fate of our planet. It is our consent to the exploitation of fear and uncertainty that makes us complicit in inflicting physical or spiritual death on our selves or others. Our fretful search for certainty becomes a search for numb complacency.

But faith challenges this complacency. Faith is not about suspending critique but about exercising it as it issues from a silent space of love, a reality yet unseen (Hebrews 11:1). Faith is about finding security in insecurity, the realisation that unless we work hard to maintain a hole in the heavens[9] by which the closed universe of anxiety is breached, the fate of everything in our created world will be determined by the human fear of 'death'.

The Christian antidote to the fear of death is summed up in Philippians 2:5–11, often known as the 'kenotic hymn'. Paul's preface is succinct: our problems originate in our anxieties. Their resolution, says Paul, is to 'let the same *mind* be in you that was in Christ Jesus…' (v. 5, my emphasis).

Christ takes on the burden of our human self-consciousness but is never trapped by its anxieties. He never loses the clarity of his gaze on the Father, the secret exchange of love in faith. Both the Hebrew Bible and the New Testament gather this gaze and all that it implies into the single word 'behold'. Sadly, this word has vanished from modern translations of the Bible and the liturgy, and with it has vanished the most important message that Christianity or any other religion has to offer.

'Behold' is *the* marker word throughout the Bible. It signals shifting perspective, the holding together or even the conflating of radically different points of view. It indicates the moment when the language of belief is silenced by the exaltation of faith as these paradoxical perspectives are brought together and generate, as it were, an explosion of silence and light. This silence holds us in thrall, in complete self-forgetfulness. Our settled accounting of ordinary matters is shattered and falls into nothing as light breaks upon us. Beholding is not confined to monastic cells; it is the wellspring of ordinary life transfigured.

Enough for him, whom cherubim
Worship night and day,
A breastful of milk,
And a mangerful of hay:
Enough for Him whom Angels
Fall down before,
The ox and ass and camel
Which adore.

Julian of Norwich understands the importance of the word 'behold'. Her *Revelations of Divine Love* is an explication of this single word. 'Behold' is profoundly theological. It describes a reciprocal holding in being, the humility of God sharing the divine nature with what it creates. God, the creator of all, God who is beyond being, in humility allows us, created beings, to hold God in being in space and time, even as God is sustaining us in existence and holding us in eternity.

Behold. Behold the God who is infinitely more humble than those who pray to him, more stripped, more emptied, more self-outpouring—and we need to remember that humility and humiliation are mutually exclusive. Humility knows only love, and God is love. The scandal of the incarnation is not that we are naked before Emmanuel, God with us, but that God is naked before us and, in utter silence, given over into our hands and hearts. And it is in the depths of this beholding, in the silence of the loving heart of God, that the divine exchange takes place most fully, where each of us in our uniqueness and strangeness is transfigured into the divine life. And it is for this that God comes to us, the Word made flesh, stable-born and crucified.

There is something else, too, in this beholding: the great commandment tells us that this seamless love applies as much to our neighbour as to God. Beholding makes it possible to live out the great commandment. It invites us to abandon our very limited perspectives and ideas, so that many aspects of life in community become not so much less difficult as irrelevant, to the point of not being noticed.

This living beneath the level of personality unfolds without denying or wasting any of the richness of the human person; it brings us, in our entirety, warts and all, to fullness. To behold God in everything is the antidote to frenetic activity, to stress and busyness. It enables us to live from, continually return to and dwell in the depth of silent communion with God. And as this is something God does in us, we have only to allow it, to cease our striving and behold.

It might be helpful to realise that we are already in that stillness by virtue of the divine indwelling, and it is the thoughts and distractions that drag us away from it. This stillness is the very stillness of the heart of God, which resides in the realm of beholding in itself. We bring everything to it, and we draw everything from it. As we come to the manger, high and low, rich and poor, each brings a gift. Gospel accounts and legends recount a multitude of gifts but there is one that we share in common, without exception, which each of us bears to the radiant child, and that is suffering—the devastated suffering of those shattered by war; the sorrowful suffering of those who mourn; the anguished suffering of the abused; the hungry suffering of the poor; the hollow suffering of the rich; the interior suffering that is the simple longing that burns for God.

Behold! He is coming with the clouds and everyone shall see him. Behold! The Lamb of God. Behold! The hour comes. Behold!

I bring you good tidings. Behold! The Lion of Judah. Behold! I am laying in Zion a foundation stone. Behold! I am sending a messenger. Behold! The bridegroom comes. Behold! I show you a mystery. Behold! The tabernacle of God is within you.

Behold! You shall conceive. It is in the beholding itself that Mary conceives, and we also. It is in this self-forgetful beholding, this eternity of love gazing on Love, of Love holding love in being, that all salvation history occurs. The words in the sentence that come after 'behold' in the angel's announcement are for those who do not behold, who are still chained by the imperious noise of those who wield power and control by means of the fear of death. The Word yearns with the promises of God, if only we will turn and behold and, in that beholding, be healed.

Behold: behold, and all the rest will be added unto you. 'Behold,' says the angel. It is in the consent to behold, the fiat, that our fear is transmuted into love.

The beholdings that irrupt as annunciations are profoundly dislocating events, whether to the shepherds, to Mary, to Isaiah or to us. They are sudden; they take us by surprise, often in the least likely circumstances. When we realise that something beyond our knowing has happened, we may be at first incredulous or even embarrassed. But when we realise that we can no longer dismiss the evidence—the traces left from an encounter hidden even from our selves—we are filled with awe.

Annunciations leave us with a sense of strangeness, for we cannot wrap our minds round what has happened. They cannot be circumscribed by concept or by the self-reflexive interpretation we call 'experience'. They are too wonderful, they are beyond what we can ask or imagine, and in their wake life never again will be the same. Yet by welcoming this homely strangeness of God in beholding, we learn to welcome the strangeness of our neighbour and, indeed, the strangeness of our selves.

If we embrace these annunciations—and we ignore them at our peril—we come finally to dread, to a forced choice: to remain in this state of alienation, to seek anaesthesia, or to plunge deeper into faith, into unknowing, relinquishing every preconception, every idea, image and notion we have, including those about God and about our selves, so that these annunciations may change and integrate us.

God, and the fathomless vision that God longs to give, will never fail. It requires only the opening of our hearts for God to purify with the fire of love; God whose thoughts and ways are not ours. Christ's peace is utterly simple, a simplicity that can never be comprehended, only received, and through it we are drawn into the mystery of God's own self-outpouring, into speechless wonder and ineffable joy.

Therefore, in this world's night, let us enter more deeply into stillness so that we may behold the herald angels. Let us be undistracted even if the sheepdog continues to bark at our side. Let us so plunge into this beholding that its silence and light will radiate even through our own darkness to illumine all the darkness and pain of this world, to announce tidings of great joy for this day and all the days to come.

> *What can I give Him,*
> *Poor as I am?*
> *If I were a shepherd,*
> *I would bring a lamb.*
> *If I were a wise man,*
> *I would do my part.*
> *Yet what I can I give him,*
> *Give my heart.*

WHATEVER HAPPENED
TO DISCRETION?

To write about discretion today seems almost subversive. In an age when we now must legislate behaviour that once was recognised as common decency, the constituent adjectives of discretion are seditious: courteous (in Middle English, the word has theological overtones of God's graciousness), modest, unobtrusive, reticent, patient, humble (that is, seeing things exactly as they are), responsive, supple, patient—all in service of something other than self. It requires unflinching honesty and disinterestedness, both of which require commitment.

Discretion flows from an essential absence, an inviolable space where knowledge arises concerning the appropriateness of action or inaction. Discretion means to know when to leave things alone to work themselves out; to recognise when situations would be made more complex by our interference. In our noisy world we are often too quick to react. Immediate responses may make us feel more secure, but far too often they compound the problem we are trying to resolve.

To understand why discretion is important and what we have lost, it might help to address some of the history and context of this word.[10] We cannot consider discretion without its companion, 'discernment', for in antiquity they were the same word, *discretio*, and were considered inseparable. They were two sides of a coin: discernment of the truth, and the ability to act appropriately according to that truth.

Before the eleventh century, students were taught not only how to construct an argument but also how to discern the difference between what was true and what was false, particularly within themselves, and the discretion to act on that truth or not. It was only then that they began to study rhetoric, the art of persuasion by which they learned to convince others of what they themselves had already come to believe to be true.[11]

However, discernment does not entail discretion. To substitute the word 'discernment' for 'discretion' eliminates the notion that there might be additional factors outside the discernment process that determine wise choice. We may see perfectly well the difference between good, questionable and bad options (discernment), but because we commonly make choices based on short-term gratification, not to mention the frisson that comes from doing something contrary, we frequently cast discretion to the winds, if indeed we pause to think at all.

Discretion ponders choice of action—or, more frequently, non-action. It determines how we decide to use or not to use what we have discerned. In Ursula K. Le Guin's *The Farthest Shore*, Ged the mage says, 'It is much easier… to act than to refrain from acting… [Do] nothing because it is righteous or praiseworthy or noble… do nothing because it seems good to do so; do only that which you must do and which you cannot do in any other way.'[12]

Discretion entails and elaborates discernment. It has two potentially conflicting meanings, according to the *Shorter Oxford Dictionary*: 'Deciding as one thinks fit', and—outrageous to an in-your-face culture—'being discreet, discernment, prudence, judgment'. It defines the word 'discreet' as 'judicious, prudent; circumspect in speech or action; unobtrusive'.

✳

Discretion is a space apart. It has to do with preserving an emptiness where creative, even salvific potential can emerge that is beyond what we could determine by self-conscious reason alone. Within it is the possibility of harmonious integration of every aspect of our lives, a potential that is brought to bear on every decision to act or refrain from acting. Within this space are silence, stillness and waiting. Discretion is what Aristotle referred to as the space where virtue is found.[13]

Jesus gives a perfect example of discretion when he is confronted with the woman taken in the very act of adultery. He is entirely aware of the many agendas that her accusers bring along with her. He knows that he holds someone's life, perhaps many lives, in his hands. He is silent. He squats and writes in the dust. (Much ink has been spilt speculating on what he wrote, from doodles to the names of the mistresses of the accusers.)

But the accusers—'the devil' is 'the accuser'—cannot bear Jesus' silence. They force the issue and, by doing so, elicit one of the great rejoinders of all time. Jesus stands up. 'Let anyone among you who is without sin be the first to throw a stone at her.' (One hears, perhaps, a quiet, quizzical, ironic voice.) He squats again and resumes his writing. After the men have left, he stands to address the woman. 'Woman, where are they? Has no one condemned you? … Neither do I condemn you. Go your way, and from now on do not sin again' (John 8:7, 10–11).

Jesus could have taken sides. He could have thrown the first stone to his political advantage. He could have blasted the scribes and Pharisees for their hypocrisy. He could have allowed himself the short-term, personal gratification of inflaming petty factionalism for his own benefit. He could have ignored the woman after the men went away, which would have been proper protocol in his time. But Jesus' discretion brings the resolution of the situation to a completely different and far more profound and relevant level. No one is condemned but no one can go away unashamed, either. By simply creating a space where all the resonances of the situation can amplify one another, Jesus has chosen to enable the potential for a greater good.

✳

The present Archbishop of Canterbury, Rowan Williams, took office at one of the most difficult periods of history for the Anglican Communion. He set aside his own preferences in order to keep all sides talking and, more importantly, to try to get them truly to listen to one another. He kept silence, eschewing empty public statements, when many people thought he should have spoken in support of one faction or another.

After the General Convention of the Episcopal Church in the United States elected a woman primate,[14] while in the same moment the Church of England was still debating whether it would allow women bishops at all, or even whether a woman bishop were possible, the Archbishop deemed the time appropriate to speak. But rather than promulgating a *diktat*, which in any event would have been inappropriate to the largely symbolic jurisdiction of his office, he issued some 'reflections', which amounted to neither a judgment nor a proposal, nor a declaration. His words were exactly what he said they were: reflections, no more, no less.

His rationale became evident the following week in his opening address to the Synod of the Church of England, when he summed up his vision of Anglican unity:

I make no secret of the fact that my commitment and conviction are given to the ideal of the Church Catholic. I know that its embodiment in Anglicanism has always been debated, yet I believe that the vision of Catholic sacramental unity without centralisation or coercion is one that we have witnessed to at our best and still need to work at. That is why a concern for unity—for unity (I must repeat this yet again) as a means to living in the truth—is not about placing the survival of an institution above the demands of conscience, God forbid. It is a question of how we work out, faithfully, attentively, obediently, what we need to do and say in order to remain within sight and sound of each other in the fellowship to which Christ has called us. It has never been easy and it isn't now. But it is the call that matters, and that sustains us together in the task.[15]

'How we work out, faithfully, attentively, obediently, what we need to do and say…'—this is an instruction in learning discretion. Williams does not use these words casually; they arise from a lifetime's study of classical and Christian tradition. All three adverbs point to a discretion that arises from a matrix of silence.

'Faithfully' means releasing our tightly held prejudices and opinions concerning the way the world should work; such opinions can reflect only a small and blinkered aspect of truth. Faith is the acknowledgment that there is a larger vision than we can ask or imagine, and the willingness to be taken into it.

'Attentively' means not only listening but listening at a level of receptive responsiveness, allowing the words of the other to reach deeply into our hearts so that we may behold, however obliquely, the vast mystery towards which they gesture, the mystery of the human person, which is as deep as the mystery of the God whose nature each of us shares.

'Obediently', in its root sense, is the attentive listening of the heart that Christ teaches (Philippians 2:5–11). In other words, 'putting on the mind of Christ' is the refusal to grasp or claim our prejudices, an attempt at possession that gives us an illusory sense of our own omnipotence and creates interior noise that impedes listening. Instead, obedience entails a continually expanding self-knowledge, a heart that knows there is nothing good or evil of which it is not capable, a heart that longs for conversion from the conviction of its own judgment to being filled with the spacious perspective of the mind of a merciful God.

Discretion cannot be taught; it is supremely mimetic; it is learned by example. This mimesis is especially clear in the desert tradition. The seeker divides his or her time, more or less, half in the cell and half taking counsel with the elders, who are exemplars of discretion. One learns from such people not so much by baring one's thoughts, although this practice is often mentioned, but far more by absorbing the elders' example through a kind of spiritual osmosis.

When one visits an elder, perhaps the light of charism is lit, perhaps it is not. Often the disciple lacks the discernment to recognise the light, even less the discretion to receive it. His mind is too full of his own ideas. The abba or amma may offer food or not, may allow the seeker to stay or not, most probably will not speak. On the other hand, the disciple may receive a word to do the best she can, to eat when she is hungry, and sleep when she is sleepy, and pray as she is able. On rare occasions, the disciple might be allowed to stay and imitate in silence what the elder does.

Discretion is not always what our genteel sensibilities might expect. Abba Abraham left the desert to go to the brothel where his niece had immured herself after being raped. He paid the brothel keeper for her time, ostensibly for sex but in reality to persuade her of her continuing worth as a human person, no matter what she had suffered, and of God's loving welcome, and his.[16]

The desert tradition reveals that discretion is not simply a skill; it is more like an art, the creation of an atmosphere where new connections can be made. We learn this art by repeated immersion in the resurrection to be found in the silence of receptive waiting, in the spaciousness of God, which is the true wellspring of our lives and our truth.

We have forgotten that the school of discretion has always been found in fidelity to our own core silence. Silence has become so alien to institutional practice that the Archbishop's discretion, described earlier, was not recognised as such even by most of his fellow clerics. Indeed, religion today is not, generally speaking, a place where one would look for discretion. For the most part, religion has become indistinguishable from the culture, polarised between 'extreme' (fundamentalism) on the one hand and 'whatever' (vague, fuzzy, warm feelings) on the other. The cultivation of a pressure-free space where faith can grow without distortion appears to be a notion almost entirely foreign to contemporary religious hustle and bustle.

The present state of affairs is not unique. For example, the author of the 14th-century *Cloud of Unknowing*, a master of discretion, writes to a reluctant disciple:

I say all this to let you see how far you still are from knowing truly your own interior dispositions; and second to give you warning not to surrender to nor follow too quickly in inexperience, the unusual movements of your heart, for fear of illusion. I say all this to explain to you what my opinion is of you and your stirrings, as you have asked me. For I feel that you are over inclined and too eagerly disposed toward these sudden impulses for extraordinary practices, and very swift to seize upon them when they come. And that is very dangerous.[17]

How far this mentality is from the 21st-century attitude, 'If it feels good, do it', that often passes for discernment; from narcissistic self-regard or fatuous, overconfident claims of biblical inerrancy and literalism; from thundering condemnations of other human beings for the way God happens to have made them—all such indiscreet activities masking, of course, agendas of power and self-promotion.

[The Devil][18] *will sometimes change his likeness into that of an angel of light, in order that, under the colour of virtue, he may do more mischief... He persuades very many to embrace a special type of holiness above the common law and custom of their state of life. The signs of it are... devout observances and forms of behaviour, and openly reproving the faults of other men when they have no authority for it. He leads them on... always under the pretext of devotion and charity; not because he takes any delight in works of devotion or of charity, but because he loves dissention and scandal.*[19]

The *Cloud* author shows us the source of destructive religious dissentions in our own day. It is a mentality that arises from the sloth of yielding to distraction (medieval people would say 'fornication'), of indiscretion and the idolatry of 'experience'. He is perhaps glossing Matthew 12:34–35: 'For out of the abundance of the heart the mouth speaks. The good person brings good things out of a good treasure, and the evil person brings evil things out of an evil treasure.' In every age, religious demagogues—and, in ours, atheistic ones as well—are quick to censure people and situations they not only do not understand but also refuse to understand. This deliberate closing of the mind is not only culpable; it exposes bitter, narrow hearts that lust for power. This kind of judgmentalism is at the root of much of the evil abroad in today's world.

If we are to recover discretion in our lives and in our world before our heedlessness makes our planet uninhabitable at any level—physical, moral or spiritual—we must start by choosing silent, receptive awareness, 'the hidden love offered in purity of spirit', which is God's working in us.[20] But we face a Herculean task. To merely begin even to attempt to alter our knee-jerk response of anaesthetising our sin and pain to make room for this working in us requires extreme cultural ascesis.

To make space for God means examining every daily pressure to which we are exposed, both the pressures from within our selves and those that we receive from others, allowing each to fall away unexercised. It is in this pressure-free space that discretion is born. This space is not 'my space' but a space in which the mystery of the other and of our selves takes on a far greater significance; a space where God's working may perhaps find a way of sorting things out beyond human limitation; a space where we may learn the discretion of doing 'only that which you must do and which you cannot do in any other way'.

If… grace is ever to be won, it must be taught from within, of God, when you have yearned longingly after him for many a day with all the love of your heart, and by emptying out from your inward beholding every sight of anything beneath [that is, other than God] him; and this even though some of those things that I bid you empty out should seem in the sight of some to be very worthy means whereby to come to God…

For to him who wishes to achieve his spiritual purpose, the actual awareness of the good God alone suffices as the means along with a reverent stirring of lasting love. He needs no other.[21]

THE SPACE OF PRAYER

Once upon a time there was a terrible drought. The crops failed, the livestock died, the people were in misery. As the drought grew worse, they tried ever more desperate measures. The shamans danced and banged pots, the priests made offerings to the gods, and the children went on pilgrimage to the mountains. A few individuals even shot arrows at a stray cloud, hoping to pierce the membrane that held back the water, or so they thought. Any charlatan who came along claiming to be able to make rain fall was hired. Always the outcome was the same: he took the money and ran.

One day the villagers spied a beggar trudging down the road, leaning on his stick. 'Go away, old man,' they said. 'We don't have any food and water for ourselves, much less for the likes of you. And we're not hiring any more so-called rainmakers.'

Unperturbed, the old man replied, 'Keep your food and drink, and your money. But if you will lend me a hut for three days and leave me in peace, who knows, some good may come of it.'

So the villagers showed the beggar to a spacious if somewhat smelly chicken shed, whose clucking inhabitants had long since succumbed in the pounding heat, and the old man went in and shut the door. The villagers thought him mad and went their separate ways, muttering about the drought making people crazy, about who was going to pull the corpse out when the three days were over, and about whether they should just burn the shed without opening it. Soon the novelty wore off, and one by one the villagers sank into the lassitude and despair that are the foretaste of death.

Two more stifling days passed. No one gave a thought to the old man; there was not even enough energy to curse with the curses of those who have been disappointed one too many times.

On the third morning, everyone awoke at almost the same moment. Something was different. The people came slowly out of their houses, wondering. A breeze so slight as to be barely perceptible caressed their faces. As they stood there, stunned with disbelief, the air itself began to change, becoming thick with humidity. Clouds piled up. Energy gathered until the atmosphere crackled with lightning. The people covered their ears, laughing at the tremendous booms of thunder and the gentle steady rain pouring down and soaking into the parched earth.

'Where is the old beggar?' asked a small boy, intrigued that someone would shut himself in a chicken shed that emitted a stench that clung to anyone who went near it. Everyone ran to the shed. The door was open, the beggar gone.

'There!' cried the boy, running after a speck limping towards the horizon. Everyone pelted after him.

'Old man!' the village headman called, gasping with exertion as they finally caught up. 'Don't leave us! We will make you king; we will feed and house you and give you such treasures as we have.'

'Thank you,' said the beggar, 'but, as you can see, I have no use for kingship or treasures. As for food and drink, the fields and creatures supply me, and water falls from heaven.'

'Well, if you won't stay with us,' the headman wheedled, 'then please tell us your magic so that we can make it rain when there is another drought.'

'There is no magic,' replied the beggar, 'and I am no sorcerer. The rain is always with you. All I did was to inhabit an empty space where the rain could find its focus and fall on its own terms. If you fill your world with too much activity and too much noise, if you cut all the trees and plough your fields relentlessly, the rain cannot gather itself from its hiding places to make a storm.'

﹡

In an age addicted to 'signs and wonders' (John 4:48), it is important to know what prayer is and what it is not. The substitution of idols for faith and magic for prayer is an old, old story in both Judaism and Christianity.[22] The persistence of idols is linked to the need for reassurance, and idols can be mental as well as physical—what Chögyam Trungpa has called 'spiritual materialism'.[23]

In *The Spiritual World of Isaac the Syrian*, Hilarion Alfeyev writes:

Many of the early Fathers... did not even know the psalms, yet their prayers ascended to God like fire as a result of their excellent ways and the lowliness of mind which they had acquired. Their words chased away demons like flies, they buzzed off as they approached. Many people, however, have used prayer as an excuse for slackness and pride: failing to grasp the better part, they also lost the part they had. Though they held nothing in their hands, they imagined that they stood in a state of perfection. Others, merely on the basis of the educational training they have had, have supposed that this would be enough to enable them to discover knowledge of truth: relying on secular culture and ordinary reading, they fell away from truth, and failed to humble themselves so as to stand up again.[24]

Keith Thomas describes a 16th-century distinction between prayer and magic: 'Words and prayers... had no power in themselves, unless God chose to heed them; whereas the working of charms followed automatically upon their pronunciation.'[25] According to this distinction, the 21st century is not so far from the 16th as we might hope. But the 16th-century definition does not go far enough.

The difference between prayer and magic is an attitude towards the future. If theology has forgotten it, Einstein reminds us that there are many futures. Prayer, especially intercessory prayer, requires opening to this possibility of many futures. Magic limits us to only one. Magic tries to exert total short-term control over a narrow aspect of life, heedless of the long-term consequences or the ripple effects.

In our desperation to pray for a loved one in crisis or our own needs and desires, we often feel strongly what the best outcome should be, and we frame our prayers (and sometimes fill them with bribes) towards this end. These exercises are useful only if they help us to examine and acknowledge what we think and feel. At best, our knowledge and understanding of the larger picture, much less the depth of the heart of the person for whom we are praying, is fragmentary and provisional. In reality it is impossible for us to know what will allow for the highest good, and unless our prayer is underpinned and ringed about with 'thy will be done' it is no better than magic.

By contrast, true prayer tries to gather what needs attention and *let go of it in the love of God*. Or, to use a metaphor that arises from the story of the old man and the rainstorm, prayer is giving way into a space that contains all possibilities and where situations have a chance to work themselves out unhindered and undistorted by human pressure or interference (Ephesians 3:20).

Most of the time, we cry out to God because we feel ourselves drawn by circumstances out of our control into the vortex of a single inexorable future. The same thoughts and fears repeat over and over. If these obsessive thoughts become obsessive prayers, we are only sinking more deeply into what we fear. But if, in the depths of our interior silence, we simply name the problem *and let go*, this naming can open our perspective and may even set in motion the process of resolution in the space where we wait on

God, the space where there are many futures. If we are in such torment that we think we have no silence, all we have to do is toss our cry for silence into the maelstrom and follow it as it sinks beneath the surface. Silence is *always* available, underneath the noise, which is only the static of ephemeral thoughts.[26]

A person can be occupied at [prayer] while standing up or sitting down, while working or while walking inside his cell, while he is going to sleep, until the point when sleep takes over, while he is indoors or while he is travelling on a journey, secretly occupying himself with [it] within his heart.[27]

Intercession has often been spoken of as 'the work of prayer', but while we may have to work at praying, prayer itself is not work. The prayer we are conscious of praying is a clearing-out of our works and ways; we name them so that we can release our selves from their limitations. Weeping is often a sign of this emptying-out, the relinquishing of our efforts to control the future. It is the sign of transfiguration, of shifting perspective, of new creation:

In this density of holiness we are raised out of time to that... primordial silence [in which] all expansion, all possibility are held in potent stillness as our tears mingle and ignite with that single, certain drop from the abyss... Tears are our bodies' participation in theosis [realising the divinity within]; in these tears we see the beginning of the transfiguration of all creation that will be accomplished by Christ in and through us. Tears are the Refiner's fire; tears are the sorrow caught in beauty and joy; tears are the mirroring of the Consuming Fire who weeps.[28]

Having named our needs and concerns, we are led to understand that we do not know how to pray but that the 'Spirit intercedes with sighs too deep for words. And God, who searches the heart, knows what is the mind of the Spirit, because the Spirit intercedes for the saints according to the will of God' (Romans 8:26–27). For truly to intercede we must let go our ideas not only of what the outcome ought to be but of what the problem is in the first place.

The purpose of public prayers and rites—which churches too often seem to have forgotten—is to clear away noise and confusion by bringing us into the open place, where anything can happen, even resurrection. It is in this deep silence that we discover that incarnation, transfiguration and resurrection are a single, joyous upwelling of the divine self-outpouring, permeating every aspect of our lives, if only we will open to it, if only we will turn and behold and be healed (Isaiah 6:10).

Intercession begins with recognising in humble confidence that we are created in the imageless image of God, that the very fact that we exist means that we share God's life. We are 'onyd' with God, as Julian of Norwich would say. Prayer, especially intercessory prayer, is dependent on this shared nature.

In other words, the life we have is a share in God's life, so that when we pray on behalf of another we are creating a space for God to use that life as is most appropriate, according to God's light, not ours. In this space our life is expressed as God's life, God's tears, God's offering, God's power. We are prayed, receptive to the mysterious workings of God's love through us in ways that should be no concern of ours if we are rightly focused on God, if we are beholding.

There are as many ways of intercession as there are moments of life. Intercession can become deep and habitual, hidden from our selves. What matters is the intention that opens the space and the stillness. Even something as simple as refusing to anaesthetise the gnawing pain in the pit of your soul that is a resonance of the pain of the human condition is a form of habitual intercession. To bear this pain into the silence is to bring it into the open place of God's infinite mercy. It is in our very wounds that we find the solitude and source of our re-creation and our being. We learn to find God's new life, hope, possibility and joy by going to the heart of this pain. This is the priestly task of our baptism.[29]

After a time, this practice of bearing our concerns—and our joy—into the silence reawakens that which has been innate from the beginning. We learn that the most precious gift we have to offer anyone, in person or in prayer—a gift that can be given only in secret—is a space where they too can enter silence, where they can dwell without pressure or manipulation to receive the unmediated transfiguration of God's love.

We come to realise that in this spacious silence of beholding, the whole of creation is present and that we are given the eyes of compassion. We realise that every moment is prayer, life is prayer, and that it is our task to learn to immerse our selves in this wellspring of silence so that our lives arise and overflow from it.

Yet this prayer is only preparation. Even what Isaac calls pure prayer, a kind of wandering with the divine, ends when we are no longer aware that we are praying. Then we have entered what he calls spiritual prayer:

As soon as the mind has crossed this boundary of pure prayer and proceeds inwards, it possesses neither prayer, nor emotions, nor tears, nor authority, nor freedom, nor petitions, nor desire, nor longing after any of these things which are hoped for in this world or in the world to come… From here onwards the mind has ceased from prayer; there is sight, but the mind does not actually pray.[30]

The deepest form of intercession is simply to open ourselves and offer God the life given us, wordlessly, in silence and stillness, in adoration, not knowing and not wanting to know for what purposes our life might be used, or what consequences, if any, there might be.[31]

Intercession allows a space for something to be worked out, we know not how. It tears a hole in the imprisoning membrane of our thoughts and fears so that the rain of salvation may fall on us (Isaiah 45:8). And when we have been denuded of our ideas of how the world should be, or even what the problem is, and enter this space of intercession, we find to our wonder and joy that we are wearing the robe of glory of our original nakedness, signing the world with the full potential of Eden. In this vast and fertile wilderness we offer the life we share with God, and we wait on that loving-kindness in a silence that is both end and beginning, our source and our home.

THE WALRUS
OF THE LIVING GOD

There was a time, back in the 1970s, when certain waterways in the United States were so polluted that they spontaneously caught fire. One of the most notorious of these fires happened in a place ironically named the Love Canal. This dark conflagration always comes to mind at the Feast of the Baptism of the Lord: it stands in stark contrast with a very early Syriac tradition that the Jordan caught fire at Jesus' baptism.[32] There is also a related, opposite, Syriac tradition that when Jesus came out of the water he was coated with our sins—an oiled pelican in the Gulf of Mexico comes to mind.

The ecological news isn't very good these days. Climate change is happening far more quickly than anyone anticipated. Animal species are vanishing all over the planet. One catastrophe that escaped the news, however—an event that has inevitably recurred as the ice continues to melt—took place in the last half of 2007 on the shores of the Chukchi Sea, the body of water that washes the northwestern-most corner of the North American continent and the eastern coast of northern Russia. This body of water vitally links the ecologies and First Nations families of these two continents. The sea ice in these waters is essential for walrus and other animals to haul out on to rest; they cannot swim for ever. Late that autumn, in the absence of sea ice, walruses in unprecedented numbers hauled out onto the narrow, eroding silt beaches near the Bering Strait. Walrus are easily spooked and the overcrowding led to stampedes. It is estimated that 4000 walrus died.[33]

This news shook Alaskans badly, not quite to oil-spill magnitude, but getting there. The gentle and wise soul who emailed me this deeply worrying information added, 'Judgment may come because of walruses. Revelation talks about the Seal of the Living God; surely we could extend that to walruses.'

It isn't as long a stretch as you might think between dead walrus and the baptism of the Lord, for the baptism of the Lord signifies an ecological crisis in the human soul. Make no mistake: the root cause of our peril is that we have lost awareness of the importance of our core silence, a silence that developed as we evolved. One of its functions was to help us to survive. Anyone who goes into a wilderness such as Alaska's becomes aware of this silence, becomes aware of the awakening of subtle senses.

I was once picking berries on a knoll above camp when I suddenly felt all the hairs on my neck stand straight up. They really do prickle when this happens. I wasn't consciously aware of seeing, smelling or feeling anything out of the ordinary, but I paid attention to what my body was telling me and left the clump of bushes as quietly as possible. When I arrived back in camp, someone asked me if I was aware that there had been a bear also picking berries on the other side of the bushes from me. My friend was just about to call out when I escaped down the hill.

The exercise of these subtle senses is normal for human beings; we are made to live in and relate to natural surroundings and to other creatures from a continual listening at the deepest level of silence. But our separation from nature—both nature in general and our own nature—has reached such a crisis that urban dwellers today are subject to a psychosis caused by deprivation of contact with the natural world. This psychosis is now on the official list of mental illnesses.[34]

It is not artifice that makes us human, but our ability to relate. Witness our fascination with animal programmes on television. When we watch animals engaging with each other and their environment from their core silence, we are looking at and longing for our own lost nature.

We seem badly to have misjudged the mental and emotional capacity of animals and how much we share with them. Recent research has revealed so much about the high functioning of other primates that there is an ongoing debate over chimps being included under human rights conventions.[35] Elephants make beautiful paintings, which have been exhibited at a gallery in London. Parrots learn to communicate in human speech; their brains have the same speech structures that human brains do, whereas chimps lack them. The raven biologist Bernd Heinrich has evidence that suggests that this intellectual of the bird world may have a primitive mythology. Even the ability to know that we know is now being called into question as an exclusively human trait. And if that is the case, then what about the divine gift that allows our self-consciousness to fall away? Do animals behold? There is footage of a mountain gorilla family that suggests that they climb to the heights simply to contemplate the view. Is it possible that our engagement with animals can restore to us our eroded humanity?

In the Christian tradition, unsullied creation is symbolised by the garden of Eden, where all the predators were herbivores, and where there was no conversation as we know it, but something like direct communication between God and Adam and Eve. It is in the context of this beholding that they are given stewardship of the earth, not a mandate to exploit. The Advent readings from Isaiah recall this idyllic myth as symbolic of the reign of God in the new creation for which we all long, where justice and mercy will prevail, and where the earth and our relation to it will be restored to balance (see, for example, Isaiah 60—61).

Much has been made of the so-called sin of the garden of Eden. The interpretations of the Fall—a word and a concept that do not occur in scripture—are legion. Perhaps it is Irenaeus, the third-century bishop of Lyons, to whom we should pay attention.[36] He says that what happened in the garden was not a sin but a distraction from Adam and Eve's direct gaze on and exchange with God. This distraction was necessary for their maturation as human beings, as was their exit from the mental and spiritual womb of Eden. Beholding must be freely chosen and sought.

My own take on the story is that everything that happens to them after the crafty snake starts up the first conversation is hallucinatory, just as our ordinary waking lives are more or less hallucinatory. When Adam and Eve lose their direct communication with God, they are completely disoriented. Without God as their reference point, they become self-preoccupied so that familiar aspects of life they had taken for granted are now strange, alien and painful.

Their fear of God walking in the garden, the tree of life, the angel with the flaming sword, the curses—these are anxiety-induced images that grow in minds that are clutching at straws, even if those straws are terrifying. Amid all this angst and drama, poor old practical God never stops loving them, but heaves a great sigh and makes them some clothes.

In a tragic sense we are luckier than Adam and Eve; we have become accustomed to our ongoing hallucination and disorientation, in spite of our heart's yearning to find its way home to God. It is far easier for us than it was for Adam and Eve to remain in the prison of our projections and distorted interpretations rather than to do the work of silence that would enable us to have a life with God that surpasses the primordial one.[37]

As Rowan Williams noted in his 2007 Christmas sermon, we have become expert in 'the ways in which we prevent ourselves from opening up to the true joy that God wants to give us by settling for something less than the real thing and confusing the truth and grace of God with whatever makes us feel good or comfortable'.[38]

One of the main subtexts of the Bible is the relationship between silence and speech; indeed, one of the reasons the name of God is silence[39] is that to name is to control, and God is so far beyond us that the notion of control becomes absurd. Equally, it is not possible to control what goes on in the meeting place of God in the silence of each human heart. What we can control is whether to remain in the heedless, narcissistic prison of our ongoing hallucination that is acted out in the very real suffering of the material world, or to do the work of silence that recalls us to beholding and stewardship in the light of beholding.

In silence beholding: we are transfigured by the love encountered in silence. We receive an innocence more profound than Adam and Eve's, for we have chosen and worked for it. As we become rooted in silence, the hallucinations begin to fade, and we begin to engage creation with something greater than original reverence. Jesus, the second Adam, is our model in this; we might think of him as the Undistracted, for his gaze never leaves the face of God even as he grows and matures.

The pollution of the earth reflects the pollution of our souls, the detritus with which we litter our minds. We choke on interior noise and external consumption, and in consequence the albatross chokes on a tuna hook, the sea turtle on a plastic bag, the curlew on contaminated molluscs. Such a baneful life adores only what it can devour and lives solely for the adrenaline rush of power over people and things. This toxic, phantasmagoric pseudo-world cannot bear silence, for silence reveals it for the delusion it is. It is this noisy world of deception and arrogance that the humble Christ defeats by self-emptying silence.

Rowan Williams is acutely aware of the church's need to restore the balance between silence and speech. Silence and the unsayable are his continual reference points—notions so alien to our culture, even our religious culture, that many of his readers are baffled by what he says. In his New Year's Eve message in 2007, he reminded us that 'God does not do waste':

In a society where we think of so many things as disposable; where we expect to be constantly discarding last year's gadget and replacing it with this year's model, do we end up tempted to think of people and relationships as disposable?

Are we so fixated on keeping up with change that we lose any sense of our need for stability?

[God] doesn't give up on the material of human lives. He doesn't throw it all away and start again. And he asks us to approach one another and our physical world with the same commitment.[40]

More recently (May 2010), he amplified the notions of stability and commitment:

The Christian who knows his or her business is the Christian who has the freedom to return again and again into that silent unchanging presence—the hanged God, whose love, whose generosity, springs out of depths we can never imagine. It is the sounding of those depths that is the heart of the contemplative life… the contemplative who knows how to enter into the silence and stillness of things is, above all, the one who knows how to resist fashion and power, to stand in God while the world turns. In that discovery of stillness lies all our hope of reconciliation.[41]

And in the resistance to fashion and power, in that discovery of stillness, lies the fate of the earth.

It is impossible and pointless to lay blame for our peril, nor do we have time. We are all responsible for our earth, and we are all called to the fullness of life in God. 'Respect' is a key word among the Inuit, Yupik and Aleut people, the people most hurt by the walrus deaths. Respect means the humility that is clear sight, the recognition of our interconnectedness, the limits of what we know, the sacredness of individual integrity and individual choice undertaken for the sake of community. On it depend survival and the fragile creation, the precious gift of life and the mystery that sustains it.

Repentance for what we have done to the earth is not possible without this respect, without our acceptance of pain and death as part of life and joy, without the freedom from the fear of death that is the gift of silence, without the gift of silence that brings to birth in us a compassion that is the new creation. From this space of silence we receive freedom simply to be. With balance restored within ourselves, we are released from the chains of fashion and exploitation. In this way we can live with greater sensitivity to the environment, and listen for possible solutions to the ecological crisis that will not merely compound it.

When the Buddha achieved the openness of enlightenment, he touched the earth. When oil from the Exxon Valdez drifted southward to blacken the crystalline waters around the Kenai Peninsula, Alaska's children went grieving to the beaches to write in the sand letters of apology to the earth and the sea.

As—not forgetting the walruses—may we.

LITURGY IN TRUTH

We were perched on a cliff carpeted with wild flowers in Glacier Bay, Alaska. Below us, jagged ice towers marked the edge of a gigantic frozen river pouring imperceptibly down to the sea. The glacier's jagged face was perhaps 500 feet high, sheared ramparts of ice in shades of deep turquoise ranging to white. It cracked and groaned as gravity and meltwater shifted its tremendous weight inexorably towards the rising tide.

Occasionally one of the forward-leaning ice spires collapsed with thunderous roars, showering the saltwater with debris, explosive booms reverberating among the peaks for many seconds. Each icefall set off a mini-tsunami, generating swells that would have swamped any small boat that ventured too close.

Above us towered wind-sharpened teeth of granite, guardians of the ice field that was the glacier's source. They seemed immobile, eternal. But the three tectonic plates that formed them continue to grind against one another, torquing the ice and the mountains. A major seismic event could happen at any time. Nearby Lituya Bay is 50 years overdue for another catastrophic earthquake; the last one generated a wave that scoured surrounding mountainsides to an elevation of 1200 feet.

We sat on the edge of this abyss, stupefied by glory.

Simply to be in such a landscape is utterly beyond words. The beauty, the vastness, the elementals; there is a kind of rightness of being, as if all the shifting fragments of life have quietly fallen into place. The whole person comes into play: subtle senses that cringed and hid from the pace and noise of modern urban life come alive in alert and relaxed attention.

We had intended to celebrate the Eucharist while we were there, but after we had scrambled through the last tumble of boulders and became absorbed by the visionary landscape, our human rite of word and symbol became inadequate to the liturgy we were living. When the priest finally broke the silence by extracting some bread and a cup from his backpack, his action seemed extraneous, an intrusion. (Some cautionary words echoed in my mind: it is good for us to be here… let us make three booths, Matthew 17:4.)

If only he had simply reached out his hands for ours, or in silence distributed the elements that had already been consecrated far beyond the reach of any human incantation… But no, he was a by-the-book man, and, pulling one out, began to drone the words I normally love, but which in that context were almost an obscenity. Everything had already been said from eternity (Genesis 28:17).

Religion is an attempt to gesture with words towards that which is beyond words. It is a dialogue with silence through icon, text and liturgy. If religion refuses its servant role of bringing the worshipper ever more deeply into silence, if it points to itself, it muffles the silence. The dialogue becomes a noisy monologue; religion dies. It is no longer religion. It becomes a caricature of itself.

People living in the Middle Ages understood this better than we do; they created churches that are each a micro-cosmos, and they knew that liturgy is ritualised wilderness. Good liturgy provides a context in which our subtle senses, dulled by daily toil, can reawaken. Good liturgy reminds us that every moment of our lives, no matter how squalid or sinful, is Eucharist, our offering of 'ourselves, our souls and bodies, to be a reasonable, holy and living sacrifice'.[42] It is a sad commentary on contemporary religious culture that people think more about what they get from worship than what they bring to it. As biblical scholar Walter Brueggemann has remarked, relationship problems cannot be solved by technology.

It is not the liturgy that sanctifies our lives; our lives are already sacred, and liturgy tries to remind us of that. The hours of the Divine Office do not sanctify the day; they bring us to remembrance that the day is already holy and we have the privilege of living it. The Office reminds us that we have the choice at every moment either to be whole, to be holy, or to fragment our selves and others by focusing on one of our anxieties. The Eucharist is not a reward for good behaviour or keeping to the rules; it is medicine for the sick and welcome for the wanderer. The Eucharist is not a lordly God condescending, but a God, terrifying in humility, who meets us, as we are, where we are, even in hell. Above all, it is thanksgiving for the limitless and unconditional love that is our life and our truth.

Liturgical action has the potential to tear open the fabric of our lives and show us that even when we are most conflicted we are still infused and 'onyd', as Julian of Norwich puts it.[43] The divine life-love is ours no matter how we abuse it, and nothing can separate us from it (Romans 8:39); it is our shared nature with God, the very substance of who we are. The rest is illusion. Julian tells us that God can see only what is like himself; therefore he ignores our sin, which has no being or existence.[44] God seeks only our choice to behold the face of love.

Just as we reverence the crumbs of bread we receive at the Eucharist, so also we are given to know that nothing in our living and our dying is wasted, no matter how frivolous, how sinful, how glorious, how mundane, how painful. Good liturgy is designed to help us understand this.

The purpose of liturgy is not to distract us from our emotions and trials, but to help us gather these fragments into a self-forgetful offering that is returned made whole in the divine life that is willingly broken for us. Liturgy acts on us in the same way as a vast and beautiful landscape such as Glacier Bay: we are awakened; our pain is taken from us and our lives are transfigured.[45]

Good liturgy helps this continual yet barely perceptible death and resurrection to take place. It leads us gently to pay attention to our struggles, our emotional state, our suffering. It then subtly attracts our attention towards a vanishing point even as these memories are flitting across the screen of the mind. Gradually, through a succession of signs presenting and effacing, good liturgy draws us into an imageless, timeless Love.

Good liturgy has the capacity to lead us beyond words and beyond 'experience', by which I mean encounters that we notice, objectify and interpret through self-reflection, and in which we tend to encapsulate our selves. By releasing us from this prison of 'experience', good liturgy makes something of truth available to us, the truth beyond our thoughts and ways that is God's, yet still ours, and that is in some measure the same truth. Finally it returns us to our ordinary tasks, and while our lives may not seem altered from day to day, over time we become obliquely aware that something has shifted slightly, that something has been justified—not in the sense that we have been proved right and everyone else wrong, but rather in the sense that all our fragments have become slightly better aligned, integrated, infused with the ineffable welcome we call 'grace'.

Good liturgy, faithfully practised, is transfiguring. The best liturgies—and the most gifted people who preside at them—will tend to disappear even as the liturgical action goes forward, enabling the worshipper to seek into the beholding of the face of God.[46] A litmus test of every facet of religion, but most especially liturgy, is this: *every true sacred sign effaces itself*.

Effacement is not destruction; it redirects the attention of participants beyond themselves, their ideas and their expectations. All facets of the liturgy—language, symbol, action, presider—all should gesture beyond; even Jesus disappears in the ascension. '*Noli me tangere*,' he tells Mary Magdalene: 'Do not touch me, for I have not yet ascended to the Father' (see John 20:17).[47]

'Do not cling to your image of me as Jesus the human person,' the risen Christ is saying to Mary Magdalene. 'Go and tell the others to follow me in faith beyond all images and words to behold the truth of Love outpouring and there be transfigured; and in that transfiguration live the unfolding truth of your selves.' It is not that the images are erased; we return to them again and again in the dialogue with silence.

This effacement is the essential life of God—en-Christing— described in Philippians 2:5–11: 'He [Christ] did not think equality with God a thing to be *grasped*.'[48] That is, he realised that his shared nature with God was precisely *un*grasping, outflowing (kenotic) love. He shows us that the way forward through the hall of mirrors called 'experience' is continually to seek beyond the images, so that our gaze on the Father is neither distracted nor broken.[49]

Through this cycling of presence and absence, the images themselves gradually begin to change, as does our interpretation of them and of all our experience. We are trans-figured—that is, we are taken again and again beyond the form, the shape we give to our interpretations, the way we 'figure things out'. We replace them with newer, better interpretations as our perspective becomes more and more the perspective of the transfigured Christ. Transfiguration, say Orthodox Christians, is our true ordinary state; the rest is phantasm. This transfiguration is not of the mind only but of the whole incarnate person. Transfiguration is given not that we might escape the body but that we might better inhabit it.

•

The soul is Your bride, the body Your bridal chamber,
Your guests are the senses and the thoughts.
And if a single body is a wedding feast for You,
how great is Your banquet for the whole Church![50]

A eucharistic community is a community of solitudes made one in their seeking transfiguration in every sense.

Sadly, for many churches, liturgy has become just one more programme, just one more commodity. The 'liturgies' in these churches lead people towards narcissism and illusion rather than the truth of their divine nature. The use of the nonsensical term 'worship experience' is symptomatic. These 'worship experiences' present congregations with something they can grasp, that they can objectify, control and consume by reflecting on whether they enjoy them or not. Worship experiences do not encourage people to seek the face of God—much too scary—but rather to talk endlessly about whether or not such events made them feel good.

In other words, what often passes for liturgy today leads away from the truth we seek, not towards it. Such liturgy, so-called, is a contradiction of the way to God, of the central truth about divinity that historic Christianity has sought to express: that our life in God is not about self-preoccupation but rather self-forgetfulness. It is not a matter of whether liturgy makes us feel good *or* bad; good liturgy helps us to face what we need to face and then let go of it in God. It conveys us into a universe greater than we can ask for or imagine (Ephesians 3:2–21).

Liturgy that gestures beyond itself towards silence and receptivity to the truth of God in our selves—transfiguration—affects us physiologically. It restores the linking of our sight to the ear of the heart, to our natural state in which *all* the senses come into balance and are integrated. These subtle senses are essential to discernment, to distinguishing between illusion and authenticity. They are tuned to perceive rhythms and cycles to an exquisite degree. They cannot function if exposed solely to the noise, mayhem and linearity of contemporary urban culture.[51] We are only now beginning to return to an appreciation of how essential our subtle senses are to our well-being. They are critical to making the choices that determine the course of our lives.

If you go into the Alaska wilderness, these subtle senses come quickly to the fore. Your skin may tell you of a change in humidity and barometric pressure that can save you from being caught in a storm. However, these senses can help you only if you are listening, if you are paying attention. If you go out into the Alaska wilderness to impose your own agenda, you will die.

The same is true of the wilderness of God. It is not that God will strike you down if you don't behave in a certain way. Rather, your spiritual senses will be dulled as your attention is turned from beholding towards the fantasy self, the constructed image you are trying to present to other fantasy selves. In every moment we are given the opportunity to choose between this unreality and our substantial nature, our participation in the divine, and we must accept responsibility for the consequences set in motion by our choices.[52]

Liturgy should lead us to the mutuality of beholding: beholding God and, through that beholding, one another. If liturgical action elides into entertainment, or if certain individuals in the congregation (musicians, celebrants, for example) use the sanctuary for self-display, or if any other agenda is substituted for liturgy, then Sunday morning is a waste of time for those who seek to worship in spirit and in truth (John 4:23). In such a situation, coffee hour has more potential to be liturgical than a 'worship experience', for during coffee hour one at least has the chance to relate to someone else through words that arise from a shared silence.

Congregations need to ask themselves what they are about. Are they playing church? There is nothing inherently wrong with playing church, and there is even a sense in which liturgy is play. But church is supposed to be a vehicle that helps us along the road to God, not a playground for self-absorption, social climbing and dressing up. If a congregation wants to meet for a purpose other than beholding, fine, but say so publicly. Do not waste the time of those who seek liturgy as a vehicle for prayer, for whom beholding leads to spiritual maturity and the truth of God (Matthew 18:1–10).

When liturgy devolves from being God-centred to being me-centred, social strictures choke off the full range of human emotion. When pain is not acknowledged, there can be no empathy or compassion. Instead, every service becomes 'uplifting', encouraging people to flee from their feelings, deny their problems and avoid at all cost intimacy with the unknowability of God or anyone else. In this milieu there is no dialogue with silence, nor space for it; no comfort for wounds or weeping. There is no room for the darkness, sin and death inherent in the human condition, or for the ancient liturgical rites of Holy Week that enable catharsis and the silence of the tomb. Without death, there can be no resurrection.[53]

We need to examine each element of the liturgy and ask why it is there, what purpose it has (if any) in the goal of helping us to behold. It is pointless to say the words simply because they are there; in any event, there are far too many of them, words from one era layered on words from another that are often in direct conflict. And why do we still say creeds that failed to pacify a Roman empire that became extinct more than 1500 years ago, words that attempt to define what should be left to silence?

In the same vein, we need to ask why we have the hierarchical system we do, which is antithetical to the message Jesus preached. In John 14 he says, in effect, 'You [the disciples] can behold (*theoria*), but the system (*kosmos*) cannot behold, and because it cannot behold, it cannot receive the spirit of truth.' Apostolic succession is only one example of a notion that may once have served a purpose but (in the eyes of many) the day of its usefulness has long passed.[54] The conclusions of scholarly research are far too well known for this sort of fairytale to be credible. This myth has trivialised the Eucharist and excluded the non-ordained from the sanctuary, so that the Eucharist has become something quasi-magical, the exclusive preserve of the clergy. Clericalism prevents beholding. Baptism and Eucharist are far stronger links with the age of the apostles, and sacramental life is far more wonderful and vast than magic. We need never be afraid of accepting hard truths: they can only strengthen the life of the churches.

The first few moments of a liturgy are usually indicative of what is to come. 'Good morning' signals something rather different from 'Blessed be God' or 'The Lord be with you.' This may seem like a trivial point, but the words and actions of the liturgy bypass the rational. Simply by coming to church we make our selves more vulnerable to the ambient forces at work around us, and we need to be very careful about the language, images and rites to which we expose our selves.

While it is true that God provides manna in the desert, the twisted discourse of the kingdom of noise that too often passes for today's liturgy is nothing less than catastrophic. It has a negative impact on the psyches and praxis of the immediate congregation. More significantly, it is inimical to the transmission of the heart of Christianity. It is not simply that Christian culture with its profound ways of reading and listening is being lost; without good liturgy there is a gradual erosion of the ability to engage these ways of knowing and unknowing, of the use of paradox, symbol, and gesture that have come down to us from earliest days. Once we lose these ways of knowing, it becomes almost impossible to recover them.

If ever there were a time when Christian liturgical practice needed to stand over and against the prevailing secular culture, it is now. There is nothing complicated about effecting change in our liturgies; it does not require programmes or focus groups or notebooks or celebrity speakers or vast amounts of money. It does, however, require that we make some choices, both personal and corporate.

We need to restore silence and leisure in our liturgies. We need to learn how to be silent and how to communicate that silence silently. Congregations need clergy and leaders who are comfortable with silence in order to effect this work. We must also recover silence as the wellspring of our lives; Sunday liturgy cannot compensate for a lack of silence and prayer during the rest of the week. Sunday liturgy should enhance the desire for silence and still-prayer through every aspect of our daily lives.

We need to relearn ancient Christian ways of reading and listening. As we recover silence, these will tend to arise naturally. We need to learn how to speak slowly, clearly and meaningfully without being artificial so that the living Word pours through a reader's beholding, an emptiness, a receptivity, so that the Word speaks to as many listeners as possible. Careless, hasty speech communicates careless, hasty religion and can destroy any liturgy, no matter how carefully designed. Disordered speech can be indicative of disordered life and raise anxiety levels in the listener. The reverse is also true: a group of children in the United Kingdom were able to turn their lives around by learning to read Shakespeare to cows.

We should also be very careful about the translations we use liturgically. Colloquial translations have their place, but that place is not in the liturgy. Christian texts are meant to fall upon the ear, the doorway of the heart. They are meant to be heard repeatedly as the year turns through the liturgical cycle. The sense of these texts is borne on the music of speech or chant to become an internalised concordance, a kind of prayer wheel that turns continually in the heart. The scriptures, especially the Psalms, are meant to live in us so that a word or phrase appropriate to whatever we are doing can float from the back of our mind to serve as comfort or warning.

Listening is more difficult to learn, but develops organically as we become comfortable with silence and learn to speak from silence. Part of the education of listening (and the usefulness of formal liturgical texts) is that it requires us to pay attention to words, phrases or parables that we don't immediately understand. We learn to receive them, sit with them, chew them over, consign them to our working consciousness, which flows just below the level of everyday consciousness, so that we can be fed in the gaps by our internal concordance, often when we least expect it.

We need to recover the art of effacement. While there is theatre in liturgy, sanctuaries are not personal performance spaces, and seeking into the beholding is not about watching yourself or another become an instant 'mystic'.

Most of all, we need to learn to trust one another and our common humanity. Effecting this goal means learning to listen to those who are marginal, who are not members of the educated, social or clerical elite; divine wisdom is given to the simple (1 Corinthians 1:18–31). In addition, we need diversity in liturgy. We need different kinds of liturgies at different stages of our development and in specialised contexts. Yet no matter how simple or grand, contemplative or celebratory, the same rule of thumb applies: a liturgy will be effective only in so far as it is able to implement its own effacement. *Every true sacred sign effaces itself.*

Good liturgy welcomes us to the wilderness of beholding God in the truth of our selves. Only when churches create rites that gesture beyond themselves will they be able to fulfil their mission of enabling the realisation of our 'onying' in God; only then will they become a means of transfiguration for us and for the world.

REMEMBERING TO FORGET

1 NOVEMBER 2007

All Saints Day, Oxford, England

The English tend to approach things gently when they can. Television presenters who survey the weather forecast supplied by the Met Office use phrases such as 'bright' (read: light cloud cover) or 'dull'. Around the middle of December they start getting real: 'gloomy' may be the word for the day, or 'miserable', or 'blustery'.

The same goes for Christmas. In September, there may be a few festive items on a back shelf in a shop or in a curtained-off area that's being turned into a grotto for Father Christmas, but the dreaded word is not spoken.

7 NOVEMBER 2007

This past weekend, the first 'how to survive Christmas' article appeared, tucked away in the Food section of one of the broadsheets. Soon the 'how to survive' articles will spill over into the weekday editions; the papers seem to vie for the best psychological advice on how to cope with the annual family nightmare. In the last week before Christmas there will also be splashy ads for Christmas-free holidays for those who have decided that they simply can't face it again.

8 NOVEMBER 2007

405 years since the refoundation of the Bodleian Library

The best Christmases I have had have been monastic. The deepening dark through Advent is matched by a deepening silence in the house: the only decorations are the Advent candles in the refectory. The liturgy is full of prophecy and vision, sparks of light almost visible as the words chant themselves, unwinding their ceaseless golden thread in the middle of the night. Then the *Great O* antiphons, giving voice to our longing. And as we file in for Vespers on Christmas Eve, the church bursting with the smell of greenery and beeswax candles in expectation of midnight, an empty manger with cow and donkey and a few sheep munching contentedly.

I love the tradition that the animals are wiser than we are. They receive the unfathomable mystery of the divine in the ordinary with mild eyes and gentle nods as they reach for another mouthful of hay. Of course this is the way it is, they seem to say—how could you have thought otherwise? I like to imagine that Mary and Joseph have absorbed some of this matter-of-fact calm until the time the magi arrive so that they, too, have a time—probably the only time for the rest of their lives—of simplicity and peace.

After Vespers, supper; Compline; a nap if one can quell the rising joy enough to sleep. Then, with a candle flame scattering the light before each of us, we pace silently through the dark cloisters to the church. The glorious all-night liturgy, followed by a day in silence to behold the mystery. Sadly, the Night Office has, for the most part, been lost to monastic life: it is impossible properly to understand the life—or the Christmas vision—without it. But you can't go home again. These days, most monasteries won't take guests at Christmas; if I could find one that did, I would go in a minute, happy to scrape carrots or dust the choir in exchange for these few days out of time.

You see, I too am trying to go gently into the memories of other Christmases. They are harrowing and sad.

14 NOVEMBER 2007

This year's big Yuletide topic is binge drinking. The figures are alarming: 95 per cent increase in liver disease in the last seven years, mostly among young people; 13 children a day treated in hospital for alcohol-related problems. People don't consider they've drunk enough until they're paralytic.

My parents came from the social drinking culture of the 1930s— the Great Gatsby era. Because my father was never a sloppy drunk, and because my mother rarely drank enough to be really plastered, at least in my presence, the thought that they might be alcoholics never crossed my mind until a religious community I was associated with had to face its own alcohol problems.

My father started drinking at a young age, but it's hard to know how much of what we suffered as a family was due to the booze or to the fact that he lost his mother when he was seven years old, an event that scarred him deeply. I don't think he ever forgave her for dying, or himself for not forgiving her. He looked like her, though he lacked the tender expression that came through her eyes in the only photo I've seen.

He hated the way he looked. I had the bad luck to look like him and worse luck to look even more like her, though our features were a different shape. When I saw the photo of her, I understood that much of my father's hatred of me was the pain he must have felt whenever he saw his mother's face looking out of mine.

In any event, there is no question that alcohol exacerbated

an endemic depression and a deep-seated misogyny. He never forgave my mother for producing three girls. He had the alcoholic's grandiosity; he demanded that we match his moods; he had a Jekyll and Hyde personality. He wanted absolute control over all of us at all times, including our thoughts and attitudes. He decided in advance, and according to looks, who among us would be a credit to him and who would not (me), and treated us accordingly.

This meant that, in order to survive, I had to become very good at forgetting, but there are two early Christmases that stick in my mind. The first was in 1945, when I was four years old. My father was in Burma. We knew he was coming home, but we didn't know when. We put up a Christmas tree that we vowed to keep until he arrived. Months later, when he came back, it was still in the house, devoid of needles, with his presents underneath.

The next Christmas I remember was much worse, perhaps the worst of my life. I had just turned five years old. We were at my grandmother's house because ours had been sold. After months of tension, and anxiety levels that made beginning school a positive relief, we were moving to Washington, DC. This would be the third move, at least, since I had been born. I was happy where we were; I liked my school; I adored my grandmother, whose house was full of treasures, including a Meissen porcelain angel in a glass cabinet to whom I silently confided my hopes and fears. I couldn't bear the tension; I didn't want to go.

In spite of the beautiful old German winter scene under the tree, with its wind-up train scooting through snow-covered tunnels, Christmas morning was a disaster. I remember tension you could cut with a butter knife. Doubtless there had been some serious drinking the night before, but hangovers were only part of it. My older sister and I were given dolls and prams. 'She won't notice,' someone muttered, but of course I did notice the vast gulf between the set my sister had been given and mine. Anyway, I never played with dolls. I hid my disappointment; I already knew better than to say anything. The grown-ups went up to the kitchen to prepare breakfast. I don't know where my sister went.

I lingered, wallowing in a pool of misery. Then I spied the fine imported fabric scissors my mother had been given as a present. In some blind chthonic trance I seized them and went to work on my hair. I suppose I thought that if I made myself even uglier, my parents would be too embarrassed to be seen with me and either I would be left behind or they would cancel the move. There was hell to pay, of course. Two days later I was jammed into a chair at a beauty salon, my mother almost hysterical with recriminations, while the beautician tried vainly to repair the damage.

The happiest Christmas I had at home occurred in what was one of the unhappiest years. I was ten years old. I had been forced to leave a school where I was doing well. My first autumn in the new school was more than traumatic. I was continually sick with ear infections. They made me slightly deaf so that, when the teacher came by my desk, she would raise her voice to correct my work in an unnecessarily loud voice that the entire class could hear. I would cringe; the others would titter; I was too frightened to suggest another solution. I missed a lot of school. My eardrum abscessed and had to be lanced. I was dropped off at the doctor's, as usual, while my mother did errands. I will never forget the pain, or, worse, the conflicting emotions: relief that my hand-wringing mother was not present, yet wanting a mother, any mother, to be there with me.

Christmas was coming. 'The whole family will be together,' my father intoned, while the rest of us shuddered. 'Won't that be nice.' No response. Finally, my mother, meekly, 'Yes, dear.' It would not be the whole family: he had written out of the book of the living his mother's sister, my great-aunt, who had violated all the codes by becoming a successful businesswoman in Chicago, while his sole surviving sister had behaved even more scandalously by going to Hollywood where she worked for Central Casting. My mother's few surviving relatives simply did not exist in his eyes; by this time my beloved grandmother had died.

In the school art room I seized on clay; after a few false starts, figures began to emerge. Where I got the idea I don't know, as my family was certainly not religious. I was slow, the forms were primitive in the extreme, but for me they were magical. They would change Christmas into something wonderful. We would become a family at last. My father would stop hating me; my older sister would stop making me take the blame for her mischief. She would finally forgive me for having been born and would want to have a loving relationship. My mother would stop being anxious and we would do things together, instead of my hiding in my attic room or in the woods. I loved my family dearly; the magic of Christmas would help them accept that love. Of course it was not to be, but, in retrospect, something far more wonderful happened.

In violation of the rules, the art teacher sent me home for the holidays with a large wedge of clay and pots of gouache. 'Take your time,' was all she said. Being literal, I took her advice. I spent all day, every day in the cellar working on my figures at the workbench. I would not let anyone see them. The day before Christmas I went out in the back garden and cut boughs of evergreen and holly, and stuck them behind pictures hanging on the living room wall; decorated every surface with a spray; created a bower on the mantelpiece for my nativity. Perhaps because my mother was originally an artist I was, unusually, allowed to do this.

Just before supper on Christmas Eve the last daub of paint went on: gold for the face of the Babe in the manger, who radiated light. My mother agreed I could be late to supper. My father hadn't come home yet. I don't know where my sister was. Carefully I arranged the figures among the fragrant branches on the fireplace mantel, guardian angels at each end, shepherds, sheep, donkey, white and red cow (from the carol) and, far off, the magi on their way.

Thankfully I don't remember what the reactions were. I don't remember anything more about that Christmas beyond the joy of creation. I do know that, many years later, when I was clearing my things out of my parents' California attic with the support of a friend, I opened a box to find the figures from long ago. I had forgotten all about it, ashamed, perhaps, that it didn't resemble the Neapolitan one at the Metropolitan Museum in New York, which was what I was sure my mother would have preferred.

But on that hot summer afternoon my eyes were opened. One by one I pulled the figures out of their protective wrappings. By the time I had finished, my friend and I were in tears. The figures were primitive, yes, but there was something in their body language and, above all, the expressions on their faces, that sent the message of the reality of Christmas: that the most precious gift we bring to the manger is not gold or frankincense or myrrh, but our suffering; which, in the light pouring from the Babe in the straw, will be transfigured into joy.

22 NOVEMBER 2007

American Thanksgiving

Someone told me with a shudder that carols were now playing at Marks and Spencer, but the other day when I had to go in, dreading the assault, it was pleasantly silent except for the usual shopping noise. While I've heard of some outlying villages done up to the nines, Oxford seems to be much lower key this year. Perhaps it is the times, perhaps the economy. Perhaps I'm just not going into places where Christmas is being sold with brickbats.

5 DECEMBER 2007

Woke up with a really, really bad case of Christmas depression, not so much specifically about the feast, but all those old inarticulate bad feelings. All the techniques in the world can't take away the miasma in the pit of your stomach that you somehow have to work through alone. Fortunately I know it is not the reality, no matter what it feels like. But you still have to get through it, even if, paradoxically, at the deepest level you are also drinking from the springs of stillness.

6 DECEMBER 2007

The family residue has always made merely staying alive a very difficult task; underneath all the static, however, is something else. As Olivier Clément reminds us, we fall through despair into the hand of God.[55]

18 DECEMBER 2007

Christian Christmas seems to have disappeared from the high street this year. I haven't seen a single nativity. Christianity today is where Judaism was when Jesus showed up.

The carols for the Readers at the Bodleian were heartbreaking, beautiful and utterly authentic. The community of scholars, the Bodley village as it were, gathered in the gothic Divinity School. There were electric piano, violin and clarinet, and a choir of mostly women from the staff. To top it off, it was Charles Wesley's 300th birthday. The piety was simple and naked in the most restrained English way, both informal and formal at the same time. This carol service is always my Christmas: everything after is anti-climax. I can't think about the words as I sing, though: the tears come all too readily. It has worsened with age; there are fewer and fewer texts that I can sing or read aloud without breaking down.

2 JANUARY 2008

During the Eucharist yesterday, the words of 'It came upon the midnight clear' leapt out as if I were reading them for the first time. It's such a familiar carol; perhaps that's why we let the words skim over us without really listening. They state the problem with devastating clarity: 'The world in silent stillness lay/To hear the angels sing.' For it is only in silent stillness that we can hear them, echoing the silent Word. This song has never stopped, the hymn tells us, but we are so lost in Babel, the kingdom of noise, that the prophecies concerning the nations go as yet unfulfilled. Instead, 'Beneath the angel strain have rolled/Two thousand years of wrong.' The trammelled poet then cries, 'O hush the noise, ye men of strife/And hear the angels sing.' He knows full well that it is only when we learn silence that we are able to join the angel chorus, to 'give back the song/That now the angels sing'.

WRITING THE ICON
OF THE HEART

On the dusky blue background of the 14th-century copper plaque, a fine and humorous hand had etched the baptism of the Lord in gold. John the Baptist stood on the left of the stream, some adoring angels on the right. A few wavy lines suggested water, and around the Lord's naked legs the happy, happy fish looked on, rejoicing.[56]

In a case nearby stood an icon of Mary and John at the foot of the cross. Mary was wiping her nose with her thumb, as any peasant woman might in a moment of extreme emotion.[57] Either one of these precious items would have constituted an exhibit in itself, but the collection went on and on: a dalmatic[58] embroidered with icons in silk looked as though it had dropped straight from heaven;[59] an enormous icon of St George from St Catherine's Monastery at Mount Sinai depicted him as a young warrior, radiant with an innocence that made you want to laugh with joy.[60] In one of the many illuminated books, St Mark sat with pen poised against a gold ground, waiting for the next word of the Gospel to be given, while St John leaned his right arm across his volume and pondered, left elbow on his knee, chin on thumb.[61]

Perhaps only the Metropolitan Museum of Art in New York City could have gathered together so many amazing works from every corner of the world. Nothing like it had been seen before; nor, given the state of the world—and, in some countries, the systematic destruction of cultural heritage—was it likely to be seen again. That these objects had survived so many centuries, let alone that they had been brought together in one place, was indeed a miracle.

I had climbed the broad stone steps of the museum in warm late-April sunshine laced with a cool breeze that sent flags snapping overhead, the nearby cherry trees blossoming in full glory. The exhibit *Byzantium: Faith and Power (1261–1557)* was buried deep in the great labyrinth of the building. I walked through a vast hall, then up a wide marble staircase. Signposts pointed me through a maze of galleries. I had expected to find an exhibit that contained the usual mixed bag—a few spectacular masterpieces of interest to everyone and the rest reserved to the specialists. I was so very wrong.

In addition to icons, books and plaques, there were stone and marble capitals, fragments alive in their fluid proportion that drew the mind and held it.[62] A sixth-century portrait of St Peter, also from St Catherine's Monastery, looked out at each of us as if he were about to speak,[63] more alive, somehow, than the hundreds of hushed people who moved in awed silence through these rooms of glory, contemplating the revelation of incarnation in objects that were both the consequence and means of divinisation. These pieces embodied the ultimate that human beings can be and do—human beings never drawing attention to themselves or parading their skill but always directing attention beyond themselves, opening windows into the ineffable. The items on display were steeped in prayer, soaked in centuries of veneration that permeated the very air we breathed, while grace worked within us unawares. Art such as this is dangerous: it transfigures.

We were immersed in what one critic, Peter Schjeldahl, called a 'perspective… at once strange and unnervingly intimate'. He was aware, too, of a danger illuminated by this paradox of Byzantine sacred art: self-indulgence. On viewing the European paintings that had been included at the end of the exhibit to show the influence of Byzantium in the West—Bellini, Bouts, van der Weyden, El Greco and many other Old Masters—he wrote, 'I was shocked. For a moment, my own melting pleasure in Renaissance aestheticism felt shamefully corrupt and foolishly dangerous.' This collection, he concludes, 'resonates… with concreted sorrow, hard wisdom. I came away with a chilly sense of having been warned.'[64]

I knew what he meant. The route to and from Byzantium passed through galleries hung with huge, riotous, crowded paintings of the Fragonard school.[65] On the way in, they seemed merely silly; on emerging from hours of life-changing immersion in bejewelled and elegant restraint, their vapidity, their triviality, their banal excess made me physically ill. In the shop connected to the exhibit where visitors could buy crudely rendered reproductions of the Byzantine treasures, I broke down and wept. I wept for our lost humanity; I wept for our lost religion; I wept for the vanished vision of the divine shining through the icon of the human; I was overtaken by a loneliness so unbounded and so deep as to make every other experience of loneliness in my life fade into nothing.

I wept, too, at the knowledge that this transcendent beauty had shone forth from the darkness of a collapsing civilisation, and, given the religious poverty of our times, I wondered what could possibly issue from the collapse of ours. As the Ecumenical Patriarch, Bartholomew, wrote in the exhibit catalogue:

In ecclesiastical terminology we use the term 'bright-sadness'. This refers to a mixed emotion of joy, over the anticipated help from God and salvation, and sorrow, for the suffering of life and sin… Faith in the person of the Theotokos,[66] the Saints, the holy icons, the churches, the ecclesiastical melodies, and the Lamentations before the Lord's Epitaphios[67] were principally created and cultivated at that time. They were the strength, shelter, consolation, and spiritual reinforcement of a nation, which was in danger and later in bondage.

He then drew a parallel with the agony of the world today, and expressed the hope that those who saw these holy things 'may find faith in higher values and ideals than those that are being offered by the world marketplace'.[68] He ended with the tantalising remark that the exhibition offered that 'which is needful' for this to be accomplished.

The Ecumenical Patriarch is not setting up a series of oppositions. He is offering the corrective of paradox. Thus the Patriarch does not speak of light only, or darkness in isolation, but of 'bright-sadness'. In the early days of Christianity, the test of orthodoxy in both doctrine and practice was whether the paradoxes of the tradition were sustained. Without this balanced wholeness, we are prey to cultural tendencies that ineluctably lead to a dead end, where spirituality becomes subject to materialism and solipsism. This is the warning communicated by Byzantium that struck Peter Schjeldahl so forcefully.

Western culture, and particularly Western religion, tends to avoid paradox, to emphasise the 'bright' without the 'sadness'. A consumer culture tries to persuade us that what we buy will give us happiness, and when we discover that the long-sought object, once possessed, leaves us empty and dissatisfied, it suggests that there is always more out there. When grasping objects has become boring, we shift to a thrill culture that tries to keep the adrenaline rush going with ever more extreme sport; and when nothing else is left, we turn to violence and pornography. But here too there is a problem. As Andrew Anthony remarks of the crisis in the porn industry: '[It] is not to do with the body but the soul. It's an existential malaise that extends beyond the San Fernando Valley into all corners of the consumer-driven world. In many respects, the plotless cul-de-sac that has been reached in the Valley is a fable of our times. What happens when there is no more more?'[69]

And so, exhausted, we turn to religion, which has largely become an extension of the culture rather than its critic. Much of what today's religion offers is designed to satisfy our lust for experience in more seemly ways, promising that we will be enabled to feel self-righteous even while we are being sated. The worship and practice purveyed by the whole range of popular religious expression, from mega-churches to alternative religions, have been customised to satisfy our primary concern, which is *me*. Sentiment triumphs over emotion (genuine emotion is too subversive and too frightening). Noise and activity blot out silence and contemplation. Navel-gazing replaces adoration. There are labyrinths, retreats that resemble summer camp, vision quests, yoga, bodywork—an endless smorgasbord of things to do and experiences to be bought. But once these spiritual practices are reduced to the level of other consumer items, they leave us unsatisfied and lonely, for they further self-regard and self-criticism and the insatiable desire for more. They cannot lead us to the self-forgetfulness and transfiguring communion of divinisation (Philippians 2:5–11).

Divinisation is a way of talking about our participation in God through Christ. As Bishop Kallistos Ware says, 'God's Incarnation opens the way to man's deification. To be deified is, more specifically, to be "christified": the divine likeness that we are called to attain is the likeness of Christ. It is through Jesus the God-man that we... are "ingodded", "divinized", made "sharers in the divine nature" (2 Peter 1:4).'[70] The sacrament of Holy Communion also confers it: '"All human striving reaches here its ultimate goal", says Nicolas Cabasilas. "For in this sacrament we attain God himself, and God himself is made one with us in the most perfect of all possible unions... This is the final mystery: beyond this it is not possible to go, nor can anything be added to it."'[71]

We might say that it is all a matter of perspective, and that the transition to the perspective typical of Renaissance art is symbolic of the choices that have led us to the isolating loneliness in which so many people find themselves today. The sixth-century icon of St Peter mentioned above has both the perspective of realism and the perspective of the icon; that is, the face has the realism of a painting, but the context draws the viewer into contemplation, the icon virtually effacing itself, leaving the viewer in the presence of the subject.

With Renaissance perspective, however, we lose the paradoxes: there is always only another horizon. If icons draw us into beholding, the endless succession of horizons of the Renaissance intensifies our awareness of our essential aloneness. They hem us in, as if the painter had grasped them and wound them tightly around us so that we would be forced to focus on his cleverness. In that era, even religious painting was preoccupied with human achievements, almost to the exclusion of the ineffable.[72] Mirrors are not windows. Paintings help us to see and icons help us to behold.[73] One might be 'transported' by many of these paintings, but icons are literally, and from every perspective, trans-figurative. Paintings are the work of artists as creators; icons are written through those who seek to further God's continuing creation of image and likeness. They are spoken of as 'written' because in Orthodox theology it is the Logos, the Word, who writes the images through the prayer of the iconographer. In icons, the perspective of the bodily eye and that of the luminous eye of the heart—the linear and the boundless—coinhere. Even as they draw us into their world, they transfigure the way we see ours, the eyes of divinity through our mortal flesh. These images open windows between the world that is seen and temporal and that which is unseen and eternal, windows that bring the viewer into the presence of Christ and the communion of saints. The icon is a sacred text that sends the Word into the ends of the earth—providing a corrective when the paradoxes have not been sustained, a clarified vision of reality.

The fundamental sustaining paradox Christ revealed is that humanity is both human and divine; there is no humanity without divinity. Christians speak of this truth as 'incarnation'. The consequences of ignoring this paradox are dire; we have only to look around us to see them. In this post-Christian (some would say post-human) world, icons no longer signify the image and likeness of God; we no longer perceive the innate sacredness within all creation. In the mind of most people today, icons have been reduced to navigation graphics on our computers. They are the means by which we are penetrated by the violent, explicit and degrading acts, images and language that saturate our technological cultural milieu.

It is precisely because of this pillage that, in our age, the writing of icons, the process of incarnation, is needed more than ever; icons are windows that show us our original face, our divinity, thus allowing us to live the fullness of our humanity. And this divinity is humility.

Christ Jesus, who, though he was in the form of God, did not regard equality with God a thing to be grasped, but emptied himself, taking the form of a slave, being born in human likeness. And being found in human form, he humbled himself and became obedient unto death, even death on a cross. (Philippians 2:5–8)

That we are alone is incontrovertible. We are born alone into the world and alone we leave it, however kindly the hands that receive us and help us on our way. Our experience—by which I mean encounters with the world that we notice and the way we interpret these encounters—is unique; no one can ever know exactly what it is that the other perceives or what it means to that specific person.

Some people, having looked into the mirrors of illusion and found only despair, die from loneliness. Others, like monks in the desert, like solitaries of every generation, seek it out. There is solace in fierce landscapes.[74] Loneliness can signal illusion or its shattering; transfigured, it opens into the divinity that is essential to the communion of our humanity. Our aloneness can manifest itself as loneliness or as solitude depending on how we represent it to ourselves: as a painting (fragmenting, constricting horizon) or as an icon (seeking into the beholding).

It depends, in part, on what you understand the human person to be. If you are confined to the horizons of the sensible mind, of the global marketplace, loneliness will be devouring. On the other hand, if you are released through the paradoxical perspective of the icon into the boundless love of God, loneliness will become solitude and solitude will be sought.

The great cry from the cross is a cry of ultimate abandonment, yet it is also, more profoundly, a cry of relationship. The late Martin Andic wrote:

For the greatest love is the love that crosses the greatest distance; therefore, it must be the worst of all possible worlds that makes it the greatest love, and that is the love of God as understood in Christianity, for which, accordingly, the Passion of Christ is the centre of life. It is this suffering that redeems the world, saves it from meaninglessness and despair, and saves it for love, as it reveals the world's truth and its beauty.[75]

This self-outpouring love has the capacity to redeem the terrible loneliness of humanity by restoring us to the full awareness of our divinity. We, however, must allow our loneliness to be transfigured, to be written on the icon of the heart. This work can be done only in silence, solitude and interior stillness. 'Go, sit in your cell, and your cell will teach you everything,' counselled the Desert Fathers and Mothers.[76] Seek for nothing, strive for nothing, expect nothing. Sit with the limitless perspective of the icon, the transparent liturgy of eternity in time in which we behold our likeness to the humble God who writes us in awe, reverence and joy. The divine light does not come instead of the darkness but shines out of it, through us, if only we will realise the full, paradoxical reality of our humanity.

Therefore God also highly exalted him and gave him the name that is above every name, so that at the name of Jesus every knee should bend, in heaven and on earth and under the earth, and every tongue should confess that Jesus Christ is Lord, to the glory of God the Father. (Philippians 2:9–11)

THE ECOLOGY
OF REPENTANCE

Snow blown by a harsh wind scoured the Black Hills, hiding the desolate plains that stretched to the far horizon. The temperature was 24 degrees below zero Fahrenheit. Dark specks among the flakes began to resolve into shapes. The soft thud of muffled hooves on packed snow sounded the drumbeats of a ghost dance, quiet voices a dirge. Soon the shapes became shaggy horses, chestnut, roan, appaloosa, bearing riders huge in jackets and parkas to protect them from the bitter cold. The Lakota were on a trail of tears. Four years in the making, this journey for the healing of their nation was a voluntary act of penance undertaken in an effort to restore the sacred hoop of their people, and to pray for the healing of Grandmother Earth.

In the United States, genocide and failed social experiment have almost destroyed the indigenous tribes. If you are Native American, you have a 97 per cent chance of becoming an alcoholic. The suicide rate is astronomical. The average life expectancy of a male is 47 years.

The ride of the Lakota to the graves of those who died at Wounded Knee is symbolic of efforts to turn the tide, to save what is left of indigenous cultures and values, even though these cultures are already artefact and, to a certain extent, must be re-constructed. In spite of centuries of tragedy, the People still have the inherent strength of their identity, no matter how shattered; an identity tied to their unity with the Earth, no matter how wounded.

For the Lakota, as for the Tlingit, Athabascan and other aboriginal peoples, this sense of connectedness and integration with the natural world, long driven underground by Euro-American scorn, is re-emerging as the source of healing and self-respect. Many Tlingit and Athabascan people in Alaska have found that addiction to alcohol and other social problems vanish when they return to their traditional high-protein diet in the context of seasonal fish camp with few modern amenities. Both they and the Lakota admit, however, that there are some things in their cultural heritage to which they would not return: slavery, tribal wars, torture.

Yet their efforts towards cultural preservation and self-determination are under threat. As the ecological crisis deepens, Native Americans and aboriginal peoples all over the world continue to suffer from the heedless acts of the developed world; indeed, they are usually the first and hardest hit. Whole nations, such as the Maldives, are under threat from rising seas. In Alaska alone it is estimated that 235 villages will have to be moved. In some circumpolar areas, women conceive only girls due to contamination of the food supply by heavy metals and organophosphates, which have migrated north. The accumulation of plastic trash in the Atlantic and Pacific gyres has become notorious. Fish stocks everywhere are depleted; the pattern of migratory runs has become erratic. Some years, the fish do not show up at all. Vanishing sea ice threatens marine mammals on which local people depend—polar bears, bearded seals, ringed seals, walrus, narwhal, whales—and everywhere the shrinking number of species points to a deterioration in the ecology that is far more serious than most people wish to admit.

Indigenous peoples are receiving increased, if selective, attention from inhabitants of industrialised nations, and not all of it is welcome. Non-Natives, especially those of European origin, have alternately despised and idealised them: despised them because cultures that have integration with the landscape as their foundation do not yield to dissection by so-called empirical study or post-enlightenment thought; idealised, because the non-Native is rightly haunted by a sense of loss that is not readily identified.

At the same time, the perils of the myth of the noble savage are always present. One of these myths is that aboriginal peoples have always lived in harmony with nature. Research has shown, however, that nature is always changing, and that people, who are part of the natural world, have always influenced these changes for good or ill, learning by trial and error. 'I become one with it' is a ritual phrase that signifies not only a rootedness in the land, but a core of pain and suffering that does not sit easily with the typical Western consumer.

Peoples everywhere who still rely heavily on subsistence continue to change the landscape from which they take much of their food: the Arctic tundra, where once hunters passed without a trace, is now criss-crossed with ATV tracks. In our concern for what is left of the natural world—and some ecologists argue that humans are now so numerous that every natural cycle is adversely affected by our activities—we must not think that we can turn the clock back or return to a more pastoral way of life. But the insights and values of such cultures can inform our own decisions and attitudes for the future.

Many Native people remark that the most difficult, often impossible adjustment to the Euro-American way has always been its insistence on separating time from space and motion, ratcheting up the frenetic speed with which we move and speak, oblivious of the damage we inflict on earth's ecosystems and other human beings by mindless exploitation. Most worrying of all is our unwillingness to accept pain as part of the ordinary tissue of life, and the waste and suffering that are the consequence of efforts to avoid it at all costs.

This complex of concerns is at the heart of the crises facing both Euro-American and Native American cultures. The ecological crisis is essentially a spiritual crisis. Insensitive missionaries, crudely trained in narrow and bigoted forms of Christianity, destroyed the sacred artefacts and traditions of Native peoples, and continue to destroy what they find without bothering to listen, to understand or to enculturate. The damage has been so great that in the American north-west, an ecumenical consortium of religious leaders has issued a public and formal apology for the imposition of a triumphalistic Christianity on indigenous peoples.

One of the most powerful aspects of the Lakota ride of many days through blizzard conditions was the sense of their need for dedicated suffering to accomplish the healing of the sacred hoop. It was astonishing to some observers that a people who had already been forced to drink the cup of suffering to the dregs would regard yet more suffering as necessary. But this was suffering with a difference. This was suffering freely chosen in the hope that renewed respect for connection with massacred ancestors, undertaken voluntarily at personal cost in a sacred landscape, would breathe a new spirit into the People, and restore pain itself to its proper place and perspective. It would enable them symbolically to move through their centuries of degradation to renewal, instead of continuing in the Euro-American way by seeking refuge in drink, self-hatred, aggression or oblivion.

Suffering and the gift of its transfiguration in the love of Christ is at the heart of Christianity. Pain is the source of compassion, and compassion shifts our perspective on pain, which frees us from fear. For pain to be transfigured, it must first be owned. The refusal to accept this truth, the denial of pain, is part of the 'secularisation' by which Christianity has lost its heart, and is one of the sources of its decline in the West. The possibility of escape from the narrow and violent world that the denial of pain creates is becoming more and more problematic. It is precisely this artificial environment that keeps us from returning to ourselves to find out who we really are.

Repentance, supremely, is about being restored to ourselves (Luke 15:17). We are caught in a vicious cycle: the more artificial our world, the more out of touch we are with our selves, with pain that reveals not only our unfolding truth but is also the wellspring of compassion. The more we are out of touch with pain, the more afraid of it we become. If our perception of chicken is that it comes from the supermarket shelf neatly wrapped, there is no possibility of resolving the fundamental conundrum every human being must work through: that all life feeds on other life.

As the dissociation of time from space and motion increases, education and religion become more focused on utility and technology. In consequence there is a proportional devaluation of what cannot be quantified. The most important qualities of our lives fall into this category: beauty, love, intuition, appreciation, contemplation, memory, history and a host of other intangibles, the qualities that make us human. There is evidence that these qualities are being eroded. The ability to empathise among high school students is 40 per cent less in the generation of 2010 than in the previous generation. There are urgent practical problems as well: how does a planning commission weigh the data pointing to the construction of a functional yet ugly bridge against the more expensive option of preserving a historic structure that blends into and even enhances the landscape? How is society to measure the potentially adverse effects of the less costly option on the morale and consequently on the economy of the community?

The pain that gives us self-knowledge, pain that is willingly sought out, examined with ruthless honesty and moved through, is at the heart of repentance of any kind. Pain is the synapse, the open space—one meaning of the Hebrew word for salvation (Psalm 31:8)—the point of intersection and integration of our selves with one another and all the creation. It is pain that strips away the artifice by which we hide from ourselves, one another, the destruction of the natural world and our indwelling with God. The ecological crisis is worsening because we have the tendency to choose what seems to be the cheaper and more painless option. We refuse to face what appears to us as the greater financial and personal cost of living more cautiously and generously. In fact, this refusal is leading to bankruptcy: greed, licence, the attitude that the earth is something we have the right to dominate and exploit. We do not want to endure the enormous effort involved to rethink and reorganise human life on a peaceful and sustainable basis.

Most of all, we resist acknowledging the tissue of life, how to move through the pain of humility to risk compassion and an unknown transfiguration, to know ourselves as only one among many components of an intricate web of life. We do not want to acknowledge that there is something potentially askew and destructive at a fundamental level within each one of us that needs examination, reorientation and constant vigilance. We do not want to abandon our 'use and discard' approach to people as well as the material world. By laying waste to untrammelled landscapes, we destroy the environment in which pain can become part of something larger than itself.

To return to ourselves, to receive the gift of ourselves—*all* of ourselves, body and soul, inner and outer—to repent of our destruction of the gift of creation, we need to remember that all humanity, not just the groups we designate as 'Native American' or 'aboriginal', evolved as an integral part of a planetary ecosystem. In spite of the claims of some aboriginal people, in a sort of reverse racism, who say that Euro-Americans cannot possibly understand these things, somewhere within the most jaded urban dweller are the dormant sensibilities with which human beings are equipped to survive, to flourish in the wilderness. It is these sensibilities that we must reawaken through repentance if we are to be able not only to survive but to flourish in the coming time of austerity—*and it is coming.*

In wilderness, focus is necessarily away from oneself. In Western urban society, narcissism is the norm. In wilderness there is little distinction between inner and outer: the human being is as much prey as predator and must be aware accordingly. By contrast, urban living attempts to eliminate every possible form of danger and pain so that people perceive them as problems to be managed, numbed or ignored, a stance that obliterates awareness of the wider ecological situation.

Prophets and holy people in every culture have warned against this blinkered perspective. It is perhaps no accident that interest in the contemplative life seems to rise during these times of urban crisis. There is a paradox here: the path of repentance begins with self-knowledge and leads to self-forgetfulness. The narcissistic thirst for 'fulfilment' is annihilated by compassion, which helps us relinquish both desire for particular experience and the fear of death.

The perennial use of wilderness as religious metaphor is rooted in the spiritual reality of the seamlessness of inner and outer. For those willing to undertake the true path of repentance, there is a startling reawakening of atrophied senses. It is this awakening that each individual must seek if we are to repent for what we have done to our earth and its biosphere, not to mention the possibility of having a future.

The most common and basic form of repentance is stimulated by utilitarian fear, but its apotheosis is joy. Isaac of Nineveh says:

There is a humility which comes out of fear, and there is a humility which comes from the fervent love of God. The persons who are humble out of fear are possessed of modesty in their members, a right ordering of their senses, and a heart that is contrite at all times. But the persons who are humble out of joy are possessed of great exuberance and open and irrepressible hearts.[77]

By embracing the pain of our mortality, we discover that immortality is not created by our ego but is a gift of God by incarnation through the creation, that God's act is not a movement by which the divinity takes on humility, but that humility is divinity. 'For humility is the robe of the Godhead... [and] everyone who has truly been clothed in humility becomes like God.'[78]

'Respect' is a key word among Native American people. It means the humility that is clear sight, the recognition of our interconnectedness, the fragility of survival and of creation, the precious gift of life and the mystery that sustains it; the sacredness of individual integrity and choice for the sake of community. Repentance for what we have done to the earth is not possible without the repentance that accepts pain and death as a part of life and joy, and the freedom from the fear of death that is the gift that restores us to ourselves, bringing to birth the compassion that is the 'world to come'. With this gift we receive freedom simply to be, freedom to hope that our search for solutions to the ecological crisis will not merely compound it.

The first version of this essay was published in 1992. As I write, it is now 2010 and the world is watching with horror as large areas of the Gulf of Mexico are polluted beyond recovery.

As of 23 June, as much as 148 million gallons of oil and a million and a half gallons of dispersants continue to turn the Gulf of Mexico into a toxic environment that will soon rival those in the Niger Delta and the Amazon.

I was on site for the 11 million gallon *Exxon Valdez* disaster. This second maritime oil catastrophe, witnessed even at a distance, has left me close to despair. The Exxon spill was a cold-water spill, and Alaska crude is far more dense that that which comes out of the Gulf. On the other hand, the rate of pollution in the warm-water Gulf, and the length of time it will take to stop it, the helplessness of those trying to address it and the criminal neglect that led to it are apocalyptic in a way that beggars language and comprehension.

One night I had a waking nightmare that there would be no way to cap this gusher; that all the world's oceans would be polluted and all the fish, whales, sea birds and other creatures, all the reefs, all the plants and plankton would die, leaving only the tube worms and a few other species that thrive on eating oil to nibble at the endless feast before them. 'Fouling our own nest' has taken on grim new parameters. We are suddenly awakening, much too late, to the fact that we have been gorging at Belteshazzar's table, that the blind pursuit of greed has made us the skeletons at the feast.

At some future point in time, tar balls from a warm-water spill— if not from the Gulf of Mexico then from some other blow-out— will show up in Alaska waters to mingle with the crud left from the *Exxon Valdez*. Perhaps only then will we wake up to the fact that the oil barons have managed to pollute the entire planet through their avarice and carelessness; for it is inevitable that those drilling into the unknown, under ever more extreme circumstances, will trigger further catastrophes. And how long after that can human beings survive?

Of course we are all implicated, all of us who use petroleum in any form; all of us who waste; all of us who refuse to repent and live more simply; all of us who have failed to insist that governments clamp down on this industry run amok instead of going to bed with it. With BP's appalling safety record in Alaska, for example, its failure to maintain the pipeline causing spills of hundreds of thousands of gallons on to the fragile tundra, why were they ever allowed to drill this well? Why were they allowed to drill when so little is known about the oceans and geology at these depths? Why is Exxon still in business, or any of the oil companies that have left entire geographical areas drowning in toxic goo?

How do we contain this evil, in business, in government and in ourselves?

What will it take to make us repent, to rise up and say, '*Enough*'?

PRACTICAL ADORATION[79]

'Practical adoration' may seem a self-contradictory phrase: after all, adoration is the self-forgetful and entirely gratuitous worship of God—not for any attribute, reason, need or desire, but an overflowing of love simply because God is God. Any definition of adoration is somewhat arbitrary because it belongs to a group of words that includes 'behold' and 'silence', which are gestures far more than they are concepts. Isaac of Nineveh writes of wonder and inebriation; he himself says there is no consistency in this terminology because its referent is beyond language:

For the exactitude of designations remains valid for things here, whereas there is no perfect or true name at all for the age to come; it is simply a state of knowing only, surpassing every appellation, every rudimentary element, form, colour, shape, and composite denomination. For this reason the Fathers employ whatever appellations they please to indicate that state of knowing once the soul's knowledge is raised out of the visible world, since no one knows its name with exactness… 'We use parables and syllables, and permissible names, and words on account of our senses; but when our soul is moved by the operation of the Spirit toward those divine things, then both our senses and their operations are superfluous.'[80]

Adoration might be thought of as a kind of way-station into beholding or a trace left by beholding; there is a felt element of overwhelming love. Isaac speaks of weeping and joy, of being inflamed, of being brought to utter stillness. He does not use the word but there is an element of surrender in adoration:

Does there blaze up within you a sudden joy that completely stills the tongue? Does a certain sweetness, which by reason of its delightfulness is beyond comparison, constantly well up from your heart and does it draw the whole man together after it? And at times does there imperceptibly descend into the whole body a certain delight and gladness—things which a tongue cannot express…? But whenever the delight which surges through his whole body sojourns within man, at that hour he thinks that nothing save this is the kingdom of the heavens.[81]

Sometimes adoration is a gift: a moment of grace in which we are seized—visited by angels, as it were—and find ourselves face down on holy ground. More often, however, adoration is intentional: we hunger for the upwelling fire. This intention needs cultivating and nurturing so that the hidden heart from which we live rests always in adoration. In this vast and open silence it is healed, energised and transfigured. In this way, adoration has practical effects: it becomes the source, the hidden outpouring for everything we do, the touchstone against which everything in our lives is measured.

We are what we adore. The quality of our core silence—or lack of it—determines how we behave, what we commit ourselves to, and who we become. If we lose silence, we lose our humanity.

The hymns of Charles Wesley provide an example of the outpouring energy of adoration at work in our everyday lives. One of his most popular hymns is 'Love divine, all loves excelling', which is an exposition of the longing of the human heart to be completely absorbed in the divine exchange, the mutual loving gaze that leaves us 'lost in wonder, love, and praise'. It is a hard and stony heart that is not swept up by the fountain of ecstatic language in this hymn, which is often sung to the melody 'Hyfrydol'. The hymn effects (performs) its content in the receptive reader or singer: it brings the worshipper to the adoration it describes.

Paradoxically, as the energy given in the silence of adoration becomes manifest through the hymn, the hymn becomes the vehicle that returns us to silence. What is beyond words and images (apophatic) generates the flow of words and metaphors of the hymn (logophatic),[82] which efface themselves even as we sing, leading us ever deeper into the silence.

Martin Laird describes logophasis:

John places his heart like a sponge on the Lord's breast, the fountain of life, and is filled by an ineffable… transmission of the hidden mysteries in the heart of the Lord. The apophatic content, albeit subtle, is clearly present. But then John takes the breast of the Word, upon which he has lain, and offers us the good things he has received and he proclaims the Word who exists from all ages. An encounter which started out as apophatic has of its own dynamism become 'logophatic'.[83]

Wesley's adoration becomes logophatic in the hymn, which stimulates our own logophasis. The hymn's words elide into the apophatic even as they are expressed, the silent Word gives us voice, and the emergence of that voice deepens us once again in the silent Word. It is not a question of silence *or* speech, but rather that the transfiguring energy given in silence is expanded and integrated by making us attempt interpretation through speech, while in the same moment insights that arise from speech deepen and expand us again into the silence.

Isaac of Nineveh speaks of upwelling joy:

On occasion the suffering and pain of his heart will cause all sorts of deeply-felt words of prayer to spring up, or joy may burst forth in response to something, stirring that person to alter his prayer to praises owing to the delight his mind feels.[84]

We need to understand that the essential energy silence gives to speech is not limited to religion but is fundamental to our nature as human beings. The relationship between speech and silence is foundational to the way we learn, whether we are poets or scientists, musicians or truck drivers. Observing the world, accumulating data, memorising notes, learning foreign languages, deciding which route will be the most efficient—all of these activities require effort and focus. But the effort and focus are only the first step. Research has confirmed what Isaac and other ancients knew, that we must 'sleep on' what we are trying to learn before it can be seated and integrated. To put this another way, learning to memorise or problem-solve involves 'forgetting'—that is, relinquishing our limited self-conscious ratiocination to the workings of the deep brain over which we have no control, but which we can influence by intention. Only then does memory become reliable or the solution emerge. The more we learn, the more we realise how necessary this 'forgetting' is to all knowledge, and most especially to integrating our fragmented lives.

Isaac of Nineveh is an acute observer of the mind:

Until our mind has been freed from its many conceptions and enters the unified simplicity of purity, it can never experience spiritual knowledge... A man cannot receive spiritual knowledge except he become converted and become as a little child. For only then does he experience that delight which belongs to the kingdom of the heavens. By 'kingdom of the heavens' the scriptures mean spiritual contemplation.[85]

The same process can work in reverse: if we are trying to remember the lost word on the tip of the tongue, we must forget not only *what* we are trying to remember but also *that* we are trying to remember it. We must trust that, by forgetting, there is a chance (not a guarantee) that the word will be returned to us. This cycle of remembering and forgetting, whatever form it takes, has been called the paradox of intention.[86]

This trustful forgetting, which leads to subtle transfiguration in the epistemological silence, is what religious people call 'faith'. The transfiguring of perception seats what we are trying to learn in memory, thereby affecting our thought and influencing our behaviour.

The practical point here is that intention can deepen and strengthen the way adoration informs the ordinary round. The subliminal intention with which we read, write, pray, cook our meals, pull weeds in the garden or type numbers into a computer determines, in very real measure, our understanding and the quality of our lives. We become what we adore.

We tend to speak of this trinitarian movement—the imageless silence of adoration, the outpouring of its effects, and the return to silence—as if there were three separate stages. The dualistic nature of language forces us to speak in this way but it is misleading. The silence and the music/speech are coinherent and indistinguishable. It is a mistake to speak of 'contemplation and...' or to use an object after 'adore' as if contemplation or adoration were a discrete and exalted entity, not to be sullied by daily activity, liturgy or spiritual maturation. Adoration opens on eternity. It is the essential energy in all of them—or should be. To understand the organic nature of adoration in everyday life is key to understanding the resurrection of the mind through the body that is the essence of Christianity.

This overflowing and permeation of the most sublime through the most ordinary is a litmus test of true contemplation. It is in adoration that we learn that all experience, no matter how wonderful—even experience that leads us to adoration—is only ever interpretation: experience *is* interpretation.[87] The narrative we create that we call 'experience' always has its eye on the illusory, anxious construct that we call our selves. By contrast, adoration completely forgets about anxieties and the self as well. But the two need not be mutually exclusive. If experience—the way we interpret what happens to us—has adoration as its wellspring, it can serve the same function as Wesley's hymn, intensifying and renewing our focus away from our selves into the continual non-experiential, non-reflexive movement in the deepest heart where our truth unfolds.

As we search for the language to interpret what we have received in adoration, adoration itself becomes the reference point. As the Word seeks to express itself through us (*logophasis*), we are continually measuring these words against the subtly felt 'memory' of adoration—which is, in fact, the *effect* of adoration, for adoration is self-forgetful.[88] The words sound in the depths, in phase or out of phase with the adoration in our core silence, and are chosen or rejected accordingly.

In this logophatic process, silence itself is not only a context but also becomes a tool of interpretation and analysis, not only for what the silent Word is trying to express through us but also for our interpretation of the events of our ordinary lives. What is the relationship of this event to silence? Does it make silence easier or more difficult? What does it tell me I need to do to become more deeply rooted in silence? What does this text, encounter or person tell me of the vision of God? What does it tell me about ways into silence and what happens there? Does a text resonate in the heart as only logophatic texts can, or are the words, however well written, just a lot of empty syntax and wishful thinking? How does it encourage me to enter silence, and what do its metaphors tell me? Does this text, encounter or person create a noisy distraction by inciting an interior storm either of pleasurable excitement or anguish and distress, clouding the mind and the listening of the heart? What is the quality of silence in this text, experience or person? (This use of silence is also called 'reading of hearts'.)

Although no sane person would welcome the return of the abuses of the Index of Forbidden Books, there is a germ of healthy vigilance behind the idea. For all of us, there are books we wish we hadn't read, movies we wish we hadn't seen, activities we no longer care to engage in—all of which can leave residual images in the mind that take time and effort to dissolve. Having discovered the still waters of peace, we no longer seek over-stimulation.

In theory, the primary role of the institutional church is to provide a context for adoration, to help us make our home in silence and the holy; to open the door to the kingdom of heaven; to give us courage to carry it into ordinary life, into the kingdom of noise—what ancient writers have called 'the world'[89]—so that it too may be transfigured.

The problem is that the contemporary church is out of balance: it has the *phasis* without the *logos*, words without the Word. It piles words upon words without any reference to theological consistency, or, far more important, to the transfigurative process of silent adoration. We have words without the Word. As Jesus remarks in John 14 of the temple system, the worshipper can behold but the system cannot, and, because it cannot, it cannot receive the spirit of truth.[90] The tragedy of contemporary institutional religion, preoccupied as it is with the power struggles of the clergy, is that it has become part of the kingdom of noise. It has forgotten its task of bringing the transfiguring silence of adoration into the static world of discord. If adoration is not the foundation of the institution's service, then that service all too frequently becomes predatory and degrading to those it hopes to serve.

For earlier cultures through to the late Middle Ages, silence not only provided the context in which people lived but was also an essential element in education and daily life. Learning silence was as essential as learning the alphabet.[91] Most of the great texts of the Judeo-Christian tradition, including the Bible, were written with silence, and the practice of silence, as a given. Silence—and night prayer—is so much a part of their world that these texts rarely mention it. The author of the story of Jacob's wrestling with an angel assumes the reader will know that it takes place in silence and does not use the word (Genesis 32:24–32). The extravagant metaphors of late antique and medieval texts often interpret perceptions related to the simple process of the mind's going into silence and emerging from it with traces of the shifting perspectives that occur in its depths.

Isaac emphasises the supreme importance of the night vigil to this transfigurative process:

'For night vigil is the light of the thinking (tar'ita); *and by it the understanding* (mad'a) *is exalted, the mind* (re'yana) *is collected, and the intellect* (hauna) *takes flight and gazes at spiritual things and by prayer is rejuvenated and shines brightly.' This passage is unique in Isaac in that he uses together all four syriac terms relative to the mental faculties of the human person. By doing so, Isaac probably wants to emphasise that night prayer can embrace an entire person and totally transfigure the person's whole intellectual sphere. Nocturnal prayer has, in Isaac, an all-embracing character and is regarded as a universal means for attaining illumination of mind... Transfiguration of the mind, purification of the heart, and mystical vision of God are the fruits of night vigil.*[92]

Our culture does not operate by the same criteria: silence is rarely an operative factor in the contemporary equation, and night hardly exists at all, much less Night Prayer. Their existence is so alien to modern analysis that they require special mention. For this reason, it is not surprising that the essential nature of logophatic texts is opaque to modern people, scholars especially, and to religious institutions. By contrast, we are preoccupied with words and argument; our educational system is based on dialectic and increasingly on technology. Yet the logophatic texts we seek to understand have silence as their source, subtext and end. Their sole criterion and goal is to help us realise the vision of God, a focus that institutional religion once had but now seems to have forgotten or abandoned. Having lost these basic insights about the process of silence in the service of both speech and adoration, churches are often no longer able to understand the metaphorical language of their own foundational texts.

The life and teachings of Jesus unfold the process of yielding to the silence of adoration and receiving its transfiguring effects on ordinary life, giving rise to what we think of as morals and ethics. If only we knew how to listen, the behaviours and attitudes he taught are entailed in the silence, in the beholding itself. To go deliberately into silence, any silence, either with religious intent or for simple relaxation, we must set aside judgment, law, and what we think we know. In that silence, hierarchy has no meaning, nor do space and time. To be silent, as anyone who has meditated will confirm, we must become self-emptying—that is, we must let go all thoughts, even those by which we constitute what we think of as our selves. The layers of self peel back and fall away. If we are proud, we might see this loss as humiliation; if we are fearful of what we may find in the silence, we may think of this effacement as a kind of death, as our attention is stretched beyond all our noisy complexity.

Isaac notes:

It is not that his intellect actually vanquishes thoughts, stirrings, and passions, but it reigns over them, and they vanish away. They are not actually defeated, for no victory is involved there. Rather, the passions, memories and all that they induce are no longer there, for that person has actually been raised from the world, leaving behind, below where they belong, all reflection on it, its affairs in all their various sorts, and knowledge of them, while the intellect is taken from their midst... Once someone meditates on God and on the riches of the waves of everything that belongs to Him and applies to Him, then he has departed from the world, and the door is held closed on all memories of it, the passions remaining idle in their own places, while that person has actually been raised up from where they are.[93]

The sort of person we become and the sort of belief we develop are largely dependent on the relationship we choose to have with silence. It is in silence alone that we come to the intransitive, open-ended faith that John writes about in his Gospel.[94] What happens in the silence, whether we are immediately aware of it or not, is a literal transfiguring of all the signs by which we live—words, images, ideas. They are mutated, shuffled and reintegrated. We emerge from each journey into silence as a new creation (Philippians 2:5–11). This silence is not abstract: it is the core silence of the whole person, and within it the whole person is transfigured; for the new creation is permeated with joy, and joy, Isaac tells us, renders the body beautiful.[95]

And it was a new creation, not heaven, that the first Christians were expecting. Early Christianity was not philosophically complex: it was the religion of the poor and uneducated. Jesus the person shows us the Way, the process, by which we may enter the silence where we are en-Christed, and from which we are resurrected into the new creation that permeates each moment. Read the New Testament with silence in mind: you may be astonished at what it reveals.

Ask anyone who practises silence: it is liberation from the often cruel and noisy stereotypes of cultural context, especially the religious context—which is one reason why organised religion has found it so threatening, subversive and dangerous. Perhaps one reason Christianity was a scandal in its day was that its emphasis on forgetting and silence was contrary to those of the surrounding cultures that were based on a collective social memory ritually and noisily reenacted.[96]

Christianity should still be a scandal in our day. We need to make the outpouring of adoration in the context of silence the pole star of our lives, and, if we bear the name of Christ, it is our vocation.

HEAVEN CAN'T WAIT

'What do you think happens when we die?'

My 80-year-old mother had the pedal to the metal. We were hurtling through spring sunshine and green hills, past the long, sparkling lakes that mark the San Andreas fault just south of San Francisco. I was careful, very careful, not to express surprise at her question. Religion was an unmentionable subject in our family, a topic loaded with dangerous intimacy.

My mother's Edwardian outlook, capacity for denial and inability ever to let go of anything were hallmarks of her life, yet she had grown old with unusual grace. Paradox was her métier. When facing a difficult choice, no matter how trivial, she would worry and fret, twist and turn, her anxiety level skyrocketing; but when the dreaded task could be avoided no longer, she would walk serenely through the jaws of whatever it was she had feared as if she were going to a garden party at the Palace of the Legion of Honor.

She liked to present herself as a *grande dame* but she had a wild streak, which I encouraged whenever it peeked out of its elegant shell. The Jaguar saloon we were riding in was the consequence of one of those glimpses, bought on impulse after my father's death. Little did I know that it was a mild flutter compared with the escapades her envious, more conventional friends would recount after her death.

'What do you think happens when we die?' Her question was costly; how long had she been waiting for the right moment to ask? What had provoked it? She was not requesting a story or a discussion, but demanding a naked truth that would bridge the abyss between our conflicting perspectives. Underneath my mother's studied nonchalance lay barely controlled terror; for me, death was as familiar as my own face.

I shifted slightly, as far as the bucket seat, restraints and G-forces would allow, trying to respond as casually as she had asked the question, laughing a little at the existential and cosmic incongruities.

'My views on this subject are mindlessly simple. I think the universe is made of love and that when we die we are somehow drawn deeper into that love.'

Having obtained the information she desired, Mother withdrew into her own thoughts and we travelled the rest of the way to Palo Alto in silence. I have no idea what she thought about heaven. She was an obsessively private person and not an abstract thinker. Until the last four nights of her life, when she had no other choice, this single exchange was as close as she would ever allow me to come. To ask for comfort would have been, for her, a serious moral lapse.

Heaven has never been an option for me—at least, not the domesticated heaven of sentimental writers, nor the judgmental heaven of the self-righteous, nor the wishful-thinking heaven of those longing to be united with 'loved ones'. Most of what I hear said about heaven seems uncomfortably close to the stories we tell ourselves when we are trying to avoid reality.

Perhaps a childhood brush with death rendered these heavens implausible. Perhaps awareness of the unrelenting squalor of post-Depression slums, or photographs of concentration camps, or the nuclear threat—any of these could have turned me off speculation about heaven.

On the other hand, I am glad there are people who take comfort in ideas of after-death heaven, even people who often feel as distant from its clichéd representations as I do. One of these is a friend whose beloved Border Collie was nearing the end of his life. Jim had been a rising star until he lost a foreleg, but his spirit remained intact. Until the end of his life he radiated the burning intensity, intelligence and energy that are the ideal of his breed—qualities that characterise his companion and owner, as well.

It was near midnight when we walked out into her cottage garden on the North Devon coast for a breath of sea air before bed. Stars scattered in their billions across the bowl of the sky, hanging low enough to touch, receding one behind the other to infinity, heaven and earth in a single frame. The Little Bear turned on its tail around the Pole Star; Orion pursued the Pleiades in hopeless desire; Sirius strobed its glory directly overhead. My friend asked if I knew its name.

'... also known as the Dog Star because it follows Orion faithfully across the sky...'

We stood there in the piercing cold, caught by immediacy, a felt sense of the starry dance. We leaned instinctively against the wind created by our small earth turning at speed through the pattern.

'Right,' said my friend, suddenly, quietly, with a slight firm nod of her head. 'Jim is going to Sirius when he dies.'

Her words went deep.

Sirius is now the abode of all good dogs who have died (and bad ones, too, who there will come to their goodness and truth). From Sirius their loyalty and love shine down on us as they return their star-stuff whence it came. Sirius has always made my heart leap, but in the wake of that conversation its presence has taken on a particular kind of gladness—even as I wryly acknowledge the absurdity of this mad mythology.

It is precisely this sort of anthropomorphising of heaven—but taken seriously and literally—that puts me off. It makes no sense to talk about heaven as just another place, no matter how wonderful. Furthermore, heaven-talk about a god who condemns, a god I associate with the atrocities committed by humans, is revolting. If that is who God is, I want no part of him.

It has always been disturbing to me to see people stake their lives on human projections called 'heaven'. They cling to the way of images (kataphatic), while protesting that the way without (apophatic) is too hard. Whatever one's inclination, spiritual growth is a seamless dialogue spiralling ever deeper between the images of belief and the iconoclasm of faith, and its hallmark is *change*.

Every one of us without exception must learn the apophatic way, for the simple reason that every one of us without exception must die. It is far simpler to learn this dispossession now through imageless meditation and prayer, which helps us to 'fear the grave as little as my bed',[97] than to wait, like Tolstoy's Ivan Ilyich, until the last few days and hours of our lives.

As my mother waited.

If her life was characterised by entrenched possession, circumstances contrived that mine be one of dispossession: uprooting due to war, encounters with death, a dysfunctional family. Beyond these negatives, however, unbearable mercy left me repeatedly on the edge, so that the borderland became my home.

I had been given a taste of this mercy when I was five years old. Like all true 'heavenly' touchings, it left a trace, and from the moment I returned to myself until the present moment, it has been the lodestar of my life.

Nonetheless, I do not think of this incident as heaven.

On 5 November 2001, seven weeks after the attack on New York, there was a display of *aurora borealis* so intense that it was visible as far south as Alabama. In south-east Alaska, the sky turned blood red while it was still daylight. Unlike most auroral displays, which are unstable and short-lived, this one went on for hours.

An auroral corona began to form, shimmering rays of every

shade of crimson from the palest pink through rich king salmon, to dark, dark magenta touched with gold, streaming towards earth from their centrepoint.

Before words deserted me, I was possessed by a longing for everyone in Washington, DC, everyone in the Middle East, everyone planning violence and revenge, everyone to behold this overwhelming transfiguration. If only they could see it, everything else would pale into insignificance. They couldn't fight, they couldn't go to war, they couldn't...

Then the tears began: this is why psalms are written, this is how myths are born: holy salmon guard in their flesh the light of this blessing from heaven...

I went into the house, put on my warmest parka and returned to the beach.

I lay down on stones.

Around me the horizon arced 200 degrees, 100 miles north to south before the mountains blocked it at either end.

The aurora extended over the entire vault.

The zenith of the corona, the vanishing point at which all the rays gathered and from which they proceeded, formed above me. Cathedrals of light ascended and descended, pillars of eternity.

In some way, life as I had known it ended that night. If I had turned into a block of ice while baptising in the aurora, I would have died a happy woman.

Even so, this was not heaven.

There was a space of about three years when circumstance provided the opportunity to realise what I had always thought I was born to do: sing the Night Office. This was not the contemporary truncated 'Night Prayer' found in recent breviaries. This was full-blown, broken-sleep, eleventh-century Night Office in its ancient Latin chant, much of it sung from memory in the dark. We rose at midnight to pray in solitude and gathered at 1.00 a.m. We sang through the dark hours until 3.30 or 4.00 a.m., depending on the feast.

I lived from one Night Office to the next. Daytime in the scullery with carrots, potatoes and leeks passed in a dream of fatigue and the joy of life taken out of time. Even on the mandatory night off, when I collapsed gratefully on to my bed and sank into oblivion, my heart was awake and singing.

It was neither a young community nor a happy one, but the Night Office never failed, not even when there was only one person left singing on a side during the Laudate psalms, the others having tranced in sleep as they leaned against their misericords. The Night Office had a life of its own, and we were privileged to be a tributary to its ever-flowing stream. The opening of our lips immersed us in the music of creation as it sang the passing of one day and, note by note, line by line, awakened the dawn of the new. The night held all the joys and sorrows of the human race, all the agony and beauty of creation, birth and death—named, marked, remembered and bathed in the river of psalms flowing into eternity.

Nor was this heaven.

The loss of the Night Office has left a void in my life that will never be filled, a continual dying in the midst of life. Although the liturgical life of that particular chapel has now also been stilled, the eternal flow continues through my nights, silence singing over a cold sea.

In Alaska the wilderness welcomed me, and whales sounded my bones. Sometimes my harp settled so sweetly into its tuning that alone it played the music of the spheres. It is always trying to play, even if it risks destroying itself. That is the nature of harps.

With friends I have laughed until I cried, and alone have wept until I was empty, a tablet erased of suffering, pain, sin, joy, which together have rendered me receptive to being written on anew.

For all of this I am grateful, but none of it is heaven.

It was Isaac of Nineveh who confirmed what I had supposed much of my life: that the biblical phrase 'the world to come' refers not to pie in the sky by and by but to the kingdom of heaven within.

Once you have reached the place of tears, then know that the mind has left the prison of this world and set its foot on the road towards the new world. Then it begins to breathe the wonderful air which is there; it begins to shed tears. For now the birth pangs of the spiritual infant grow strong, since grace, the common mother of all, makes haste to give birth mystically to the soul, the image of God, into the light of the world to come… Then you will start to become aware of the transformation which the whole nature will receive in the renewal of all things, dimly and as though by hints.[98]

Heaven is without beginning and without end. It's when I'm not looking for heaven that heaven appears. It is, by definition, more than I can ask or imagine. It permeates all that I live, have lived and will live, in weal and in woe. It suffuses the ordinary flow of our lives if only we will stop trying to cut it down to our size, to objectify it, to make it finitely less than it is.

My mother solved her problem with death by having the definitive fall, fracturing so many bones that she was caved in on one side. They could not be set as she was too fragile to risk the slightest intervention. She was in hospital a couple of weeks, then demanded to go home. Twenty-four hours later she was back with drug-resistant pneumonia.

I bought scrubs and a cot and moved into her room.

She was lightly comatose, parched with a high fever. There was little to be done: cold cloths for her forehead, swabs to keep her mouth moist. She sucked hard on the swabs.

The second night her fever broke, but she was awakened by pain. She must have been in agony. In her final two years she had become paranoid and, after her fall, had refused pain medication on the grounds that it might further weaken her failing heart.

With some diffidence I suggested that, in spite of her fears, a little morphine might be a good idea. She looked at me suspiciously as if she thought I might be trying to do her in, then agreed.

The bolus hurt her; she was skin and bones. I asked the nurse to put her on a drip.

The third night she seemed to rally. She was sometimes unconscious, sometimes wide awake. 'Don't waste your money on skin creams,' she admonished in one lucid interval. 'They don't work!'

Another time her eyes flew open. 'I'm getting better!' she announced in a tone of voice that brooked no contradiction.

And as an afterthought: 'I've always hoped you'd change your mind, get married and have some grandchildren. It's not too late!'

Denial dies hard. I was 58 years old and 17 years beyond a total hysterectomy.

The fourth night she lapsed again into a light coma. The struggle between flesh and spirit seemed to be building to an unbearable level. In the small hours of the morning she appeared stuck, unable to accept fully that she was dying, unable to let go.

As I sat helpless before her impasse, an incongruous memory appeared. I had once borrowed a jumper she hadn't worn for a dozen years and which, because of her arthritis, she could never wear again. I'd found it during a visit when I was helping her look deep in her walk-in closet for a pair of shoes. With great reluctance she let me take it. About a month later she made an agitated trans-Atlantic phone call to ask me if I had the jumper and to please send it back immediately.

This memory prodded another: the question and answer in the car seven years earlier. I gathered all my courage and leaned tentatively towards her, careful not to touch.

'Mother,' I said as gently as I could. 'Mother, it's all right to let go into love.'

Her body gave a great start as if she were trying to sit up to stare me down, to negate my words. She slumped back on the pillows.

Softly the melodies she had once loved to hear her husband sing began to spin from my lips. Psalms we had read at *her* mother's dying emerged from the ever-flowing stream to sing the dawn. Slowly her body began to relax. The strain left her face. She was going to a garden party through the jaws of death.

But then a different struggle began, one more pitiful by far than the first. It lasted the next twelve hours. She had consented to die, but her physiology was so conditioned never to let go that it fought her will and her desire for every breath and every heartbeat.

During her final hours she was no longer responsive. Her eyes were half-open, unblinking. Slowly the inexorable pattern established itself, breathing that lingered and lagged and stopped and started again after successively longer pauses. Her pulse lurched in her throat, then, after an impossible gap, throbbed again.

Suddenly, on the last beat, her face became fully conscious, alive, sentient; her features contorted with excruciating pain and effort—and, in the same fleeting instant, collapsed.

In the end, it seems, the only way she could let go was to break her heart.

Heaven can't wait.

TEARS AND FIRE

Blessed, therefore, are the pure in heart who at all times enjoy this delight of tears and through it see our Lord continually.

ISAAC OF NINEVEH, ASCETICAL HOMILIES

Tears arise from stillness and lead us to deeper stillness. In the earliest days of the churches, tears were considered essential to Christian praxis. Their most eloquent champions are found in Syrian tradition, especially Ephrem and Isaac. The early writers on tears had a profound understanding of the human person. They mapped out our fragmentation through sin and the reintegration that is accomplished by the grace of tears. This term not only referred to actual weeping but was also a euphemism for the organic transfiguration of the person. Unfortunately today this rich tradition has been lost, and tears, more often than not, are regarded as quaint, embarrassing and even shameful. In the face of increasing disintegration, both personal and societal, recovering the way of tears is critical.

Tears signify losing one's life—or, rather, what one thinks of as one's life; one's pseudo-life—in order to gain true life (Matthew 10:39); tears are at the core of receiving and mirroring the outpouring of God's love in *kenosis* that begins with creation and finds its human perfection in Jesus the Christ (Philippians 2:5–11).

Ephrem, the fourth-century Syrian writer, understands both the type and the incarnation of this *kenosis*:

Just as the bush on Horeb bore
God in the flame,
So did Mary bear
Christ in her virginity…

A Virgin is pregnant with God
and a barren woman is pregnant with a virgin
the son of sterility leaps at the pregnancy of virginity.[99]

While the tradition of *kenosis* expressed through weeping as a personal striving of each Christian has been kept alive in some areas of the Christian East, in the West it has surfaced primarily through devotion. In some spiritual movements, weeping has been seen chiefly as imitation through external observance or imagination, often expressed as imposed or self-imposed acts of abasement according to an accepted stereotype. This is not the kenotic tradition of tears. This misinterpretation stems in part from confusing obedience with dependence. The tradition of tears is not concerned with imitation but with the indwelling of the kenotic Christ, an indwelling that is in part hidden in us at creation, in part manifest when we are willing to be open to God's kenotic life, making room for it to pour through us. God's kenotic life overflowed into Mary's self-outpouring; like the bush on Horeb, she is filled with God but not consumed.

What is the life of which we are emptied? What do we mean by 'the world'? Isaac of Nineveh has an exact description of 'the world' (more specifically, the 'passions'):

These are: love of riches; the gathering of possessions, fattening up the body, giving rise to the tendency toward carnal desire; love of honour, which is the source of envy; the exercise or position of power; pride and the trappings of authority; outward elegance; glory among men, which is the cause of resentment; fear for the body.[100]

Note that these passions not only induce the illusion of power and status, security and even immortality in the person who possesses (or is possessed by) them but also provoke envy and resentment in others. At their root is 'bodily fear', that is, the fear of death. To yield to the passions, to deny mortality, is to begin a malignant cycle. One lie needs to be supported by another. The clamour becomes so great that there is no room to hear the Word, much less give birth to it. Isaac is writing for monks, but he draws on an older, pre-monastic tradition.

In the background of Isaac the Syrian's spirituality is the notion of *ihidayutha*. It is difficult for the tidy Western mind to enter the vastness of interior territory that *ihidayutha* encompasses. *Ihidayutha* is the focus of the whole creation coinhered with the single movement of love that is God. Subsumed under *ihidayutha* are virginity, chastity, integrity, inviolable vulnerability, wholeness, solitude, singleness—unity of God and creation, unity of inner and outer, unity of man and woman, unity of image and what is imaged. It has resonances of the mercy-seat, the throne, the empty space between the cherubim in the holy of holies in the old Jerusalem temple, which is, as Rowan Williams (quoting Bishop Westcott) reminds us, 'the most potent sign of Israel's repudiation of idols, the great speaking absence between the images'.[101] This is the background of the birth of the Single Only One through the Single One—in other words, she who was single-hearted. This notion renders our squabbling over the doctrine of the virgin birth ludicrous. It has nothing to do with the intactness of a membrane. Indeed, the analogy that comes closest to this virginity of the mind is that of the free-fall experienced in sexual orgasm.

Ihidayutha: it is as if light is focused into a laser, or our humanity into a pillar of flame. It is the uncompromising, joyous wildness of undistracted longing and love for God. Perhaps the absolute essence of *ihidayutha* is this singleness of heart, the desire for God alone that, even given the vision of paradise, ends in the often terrifying abandonment of all images of God, all notions of God—all notions, even, of what prayer is, all in religion with which we comfort our selves and that ultimately creates a barrier between us and the divine fire if not allowed to fall away. Isaac speaks of the person 'who in his mind clings to nothing visible',[102] of imageless prayer, of prayer beyond prayer. This iconoclasm in prayer is, of course, a form of death because we give up the security of our pet ideas of God and religion; we abandon all the ways that encourage self-reflection, all the ways that enable us to tell ourselves that we are good and are becoming holy.

In the hymns of Ephrem, who lived 300 years before Isaac, there is no confusion of 'the world' and creation: creation is revered and celebrated with the single-heartedness that can arise only when theology is united to prayer. Ephrem's theology is worship, engagement with God as opposed to the positing of God. He understands that a kenotic God who points away from the divine Self in outpouring love cannot be posited, and that to systematise is to kill the life of the very God whom theology purports to reveal. Ephrem's theology of prayer suggests that to confine God to mere human reason is to blaspheme.

Ephrem understands 'virginity' as the mystery of human-focused relatedness to God, who reaches over the ontological abyss. Thus virginity, once again, is not confined to mere genital continence, but is closer to Kierkegaard's description of purity of heart: to will one thing—that is, to be willing to mirror God's life, contained and outpoured, love that cannot but move to the heart of pain to find new life, hope and joy. In the willingness to be so emptied, God is revealed indwelling the daily life of each Christian.

I heard a young man singing one day
Would that someone would pull me down and rebuild me, and make me
a virgin once again, and I told him that this request of yours is possible
with Jesus.[103]

How do we come to this single-heartedness? Through self-knowledge—an unflinching, dispassionate examination of all the ways in which we seek power, status and security by creation of the kinds of illusion Isaac listed in his description of 'the world'. This rigorous honesty is not self-judgment: that would be to assume another kind of power. It is, rather, allowing one's self to be exposed to the light of God that illuminates and burns away all that is not pure. It is that piercing light that is *katanyxis*, the painful shock that shows us the illusory nature of our perceptions about our selves, the sham image we desire to project. It is this shock that begins to turn us towards repentance, the *penthos* that is the matrix of holy tears.

We need to make a distinction here between the unfolding truth of the self and self-image. Relinquishing self-image involves letting go illusions of power, particularly the illusions that we are in control, that we can control and that we should control. Our desire to control is a trap that enslaves us, a trap we construct to give us a false sense of security from the fantasy fears we have about death (Hebrews 2:14–15). It is a trap because our own designs are limited and cannot help but end in a closed system, a dead end. God becomes incarnate to free us from this slavery; the word 'salvation', in one of its oldest Hebrew forms, means to be sprung from a trap. Closed systems may make us feel safe, but they obviate possibility. By contrast, salvation—being sprung from a trap—means possibility.

What do we mean by control? Giving up the world, in Isaac's definition, is often rightly put in terms of self-control. But this is very different from the world's entrapping control. Self-control is a gathering of the fragments of self-image into self-discipline in order to be emptied, in order to lose control. Self-image must be emptied so that God, whose very identity is the outpouring of divine mercy, might enter, indwell, and pour through us the transfiguring Spirit on to the earth.

God's life dwells in us, whether or not we cooperate. We share the divine nature, and we exist by mercy. Yet we need to open to God's grace in order to increase our capacity for the pouring of divine love through us. To open to God, we must become willing. That is all we have to do. God will do the rest. In fact, it is very important that we do nothing but become willing. And this willingness is not quietism. It costs not less than everything. Willingness is not passivity: it is a chosen receptivity, a readiness for beholding.[104] Willing for what? Willing to be powerless, willing to limit our seeming power so that God's real power can become active in us, most especially in relation to what we would like to do for God. As the ancient desert wisdom tells us, the work of asceticism we do by our own effort is entirely pagan: it is only when we run up against the wall of despair at the failure of our efforts, only when we are willing to acknowledge our powerlessness and thus enable God's power to be active in us, that our service becomes Christian.

Tears are a sign that we are struggling with power of one sort or another: the loss of ours, the entering of God's. Through tears our passions are tamed, the wayward found, and the compromised made inviolably vulnerable. 'Tears are to the mind the border, as it were, between the bodily and the spiritual state, between the state of being subject to the passions and that of purity.'[105]

Some tears cause burning, others provide a kind of unction. All tears which flow out of compunction and anguish of heart as a result of sins dry up the body and burn it. And often when these tears are shed, a person will even feel that some harm has been done to his brain. A person will necessarily encounter this order of tears first of all. Then by them the door leading to the second order will be opened for him, an order which is by far superior, because it constitutes the sign of the receiving of mercy. What is this? Those tears which pour forth as a result of some insight provide the body with a kind of unction; they flow spontaneously and there is no compulsion in them. They also anoint the body and the appearance of the face is changed. For a joyful heart renders the body beautiful.[106]

Psychology distinguishes between types of tears. Although holy tears may permeate other kinds of tears, holy tears are not the same as the tears of bereavement, whether this bereavement is for the loss of a person or some option or possession. The grief of bereavement has a beginning, a middle and what currently is known as 'closure', a time when the active passage of bereavement ends. It is also significant that emotional tears of joy last but a few moments, while holy tears are unending.

The grief associated with penitence, with the *metanoia* of being turned round and inside out, is continuous because, as the movement towards God continues and becomes more intense, the process of being organically transfigured, the process of divinisation, also continues. More and more illusion is lost. More and more sense of counterfeit power and control is lost, and holy tears are evidence of catharsis. These tears are the sign both of the Holy Spirit at work in a willing person and of the willingness itself. They signify the hidden beholding, the kenotic exchange of love between God and the person. They have nothing to do with melancholy or masochism.

Though results of current scientific research correlate with the observations of Isaac, John Climacus and Symeon the New Theologian that the ability or inability to weep is due partly to genetic disposition, and partly to cultural conditioning, difficulty in weeping can be overcome by willingness to be transfigured. Isaac says emphatically that he will not believe someone's *metanoia* until he sees the person weep. Isaac's contemporary, John Climacus, seems to be more moderate, saying that he prizes the single tear of someone who finds it nearly impossible to weep. Symeon echoes Isaac by saying that tears are mandatory. The seeming contradiction between Climacus and the other two can be resolved by understanding that a person who laments the inability to weep discovers that something fundamental in his inner life must be changed, and that it is possible to become vulnerable to weeping if one is willing. The key here is the willingness to be transfigured, to undergo the pain associated with changing perspective and new creation.

Thus tears are a sign of transfiguration, evidence of glimpsing deepest reality. The first stages of the way of tears necessarily focus inward. But soon there is a decided shift. As the emptying process imperceptibly takes place, compassion grows. This compassion grows because of the revelation of one's own wounds. These in turn are recognised to be the wounds of all humanity, and of all creation. The interrelatedness, the coinherence of all suffering, all sin and all joy becomes more and more apparent, and one's focus begins to shift outward. Isaac writes eloquently of this compassion:

The burning of the heart on behalf of the entire creation, human beings, birds, animals—even all that exists; so that by the recollection and at the sight of them the eyes well up with tears as a result of the vehemence of the compassion which constrains the heart in abundant pity. Then the heart becomes weak [literally, small] and it is not able to bear to hear or to observe the injury or any insignificant suffering of anything in creation. For this reason, even on behalf of the irrational beings and enemies of truth, yes even on behalf of those who do harm to it, he offers prayer with tears at all times that they may be protected and spared; he even extends this to the various reptiles, on account of his great compassion infused without measure in his heart, after the likeness of God...

The humble person approaches beasts of prey, and as soon as their gaze alights upon him, their wildness is tamed and they approach him and attach themselves to him as their master, wagging their tails and licking his hands and feet. For they smell from him the scent which wafted from Adam before his transgression, when the beasts gathered to him and he gave the names in Paradise—the scent which was taken from us and given back to us anew by Christ through His advent, for it is He who has made the smell of the human race sweet. [107]

It is as if the angel guarding paradise with a flaming sword lowers it in wonder at the sight of our tears, and, as its cruel blade falls before us, it is extinguished and dissolved by the flood of our pain and joy. So may we enter an innocence more precious than our first parents'.

The healing of our wounds is not as the world understands healing: closure and scarring. Rather, our wounds are transfigured by tears. By God's grace, these wounds become united with Christ's. It is through our wounds that *kenosis* takes place, and God's enters. Our wounds, thus united with God's, are the beginning of our glorified body.

Eventually we may become aware that there is simultaneous inward and outward movement, a kind of circulation or flow. This movement is as impossible to describe as the physicist Werner Heisenberg has shown it impossible to calculate the simultaneous speed and position of a subatomic particle. And we have to remember that while we speak in terms of phases and processes, *theosis* is one process occurring on many levels at once. Perhaps the closest we can come to imagining it is as an ever-widening spiral.

In the depths of tears we find that our tears are God's. God weeps, and the will of God emerges from divine tears mingled with ours. God's willing powerlessness and involvement in co-creation extends to every moment and every eventuality, and the divine mercy pervades every suffering. God willingly suffers. That this semitic understanding of God is retained through centuries of Chalcedonian and post-Chalcedonian conflict is astonishing. But it is implicit in both Ephrem and Isaac, as it is implicit in the biblical word 'behold'.

As we approach the depth of tears, we come to a crisis of re-birth, particularly in the first overflowing of tears, but also in each subsequent weeping. Every person has a sense of being pulled through density into newness in a different way. Isaac sums his up in a famous passage:

And when the time of birth is come, then the mind will perceive something of what belongs to that [new] world, like a faint perfume which an infant receives inside the body in which it has grown. Then, unable to endure what is unwonted, it (the spiritual infant) will set the body to weeping mingled with joy which surpasses the sweetness of honey. Together with the growing of this interior infant there will be an increase of tears. The stream of tears occurs when the mind has begun to become serene. I am talking about the flow of tears belonging to the stage which I have described, not that partial one which takes place from time to time. This consolation which takes place intermittently occurs for everyone who serves God in solitude; sometimes it happens when the mind is in contemplation, sometimes while reading the words of the scriptures; sometimes when the mind is occupied with supplication.

But I propose to speak of that total kind, which continues night and day without a break, and by the sincerity of his behaviour, when the eyes become fountains of water for a period of nearly two years. This happens during a transitional period; I mean mystical transition. At the end of the period of tears you will enter into peace of thought; and by this peace of thought you will enter into that divine rest of which Paul spoke, rest in part, according to [our] nature.

From this place of peace the intellect will begin to see hidden things. Then the Holy Spirit will begin to reveal before it heavenly things, while God dwells in you and promotes spiritual fruits in you. Then you will start to become aware of the transformation which the whole nature will receive in the renewal of all things, dimly and as though by hints.[108]

Tears, like laughter, their near-twin, spring from polarity, the holding of two opposite ends of a continuum in the heart: knowledge of the sin and pain of life on the one hand, and the vision of God on the other. The polarity is acute even (and perhaps especially) when the glory of creation and the achievements of humankind are at their best. Yet these wonders are beheld contrasted with the vision that is unfolding, and the coming of the person into sacred time that is interpenetrated with and becoming the 'ordinary'.

The ever-narrowing prison of attitudes of control, and our willing powerlessness, our poverty, our need of God, funnel to the point of despair, the strait place through which we must pass into the density of the glory of God, where all laws break down and everything is reordered. This strait place is critical, and the despair is not only the despair of coming to the dead end of mere human reason and worldly endeavour to control, but also the despair in which there is only God. Olivier Clément writes of it thus:

What we must say to all those who are wounded by the 'terrorist' God is that basically what is asked of man is not virtue or merit, but a cry of trust and love from the depths of his hell; or who knows, a moment of anguish and startlement in the enclosed immanence of his happiness. And never to fall into despair, but into God.[109]

For as Christ said to the Staretz Silouan: 'Keep your mind in hell and despair not.' In the depths of hell the soul aspires to Mercy, and it is there that it finds itself to be loved. This is a permanent metanoia: *the world ceases to be that of the 'me', which idolises itself (and at the same time hates itself), to become the world of God, the apparently upside-down world of the Beatitudes and of Communion. Then we understand that suffering, hell and death are spread abroad by means of the 'powers of darkness' in our hearts; but also that Christ is the Conqueror of hell and death, and that this risen life, light and freshness of Spirit, can increase in us from ever greater depths, according to the measure of our faith and our humility, to make of us beings of wonder, and sometimes of blessing.*[110]

Our passing through this suffering is thus not 'punishment' or 'penance' inflicted by a wrathful God for our sins, but rather an awareness that God is with us in the passage through this strait place, that God is suffering with us. For, as Isaac of Nineveh insists:

The whole purpose of our Lord's death was not to deliver (or redeem) us from sins, or for any other reason, but solely in order that the world might become aware of the love which God has for creation. Had all this astounding affair taken place solely for the purpose of forgiveness of sin, it would have been sufficient to redeem us by some other means… What wisdom is God's! And how filled with life![111]

In this singularity at the bottom of tears we find silence, we find *hesychia*.

In the silence of God—or, as John the Solitary would say, the God who is Silence—we come to the timeless moment where creation and *parousia* intersect. Here is the wedding of heaven and earth. We come to know that each of us is a solitary, and that the true meaning of solitude is the mirroring of God's outpouring love that, through our tears, gathers the community of creation. Thus we become kenotic co-creators, artists engaged in expressing God's abundance.

In the way of tears, we become prayer; we no longer labour under the illusion of prayer as technology. Isaac speaks of the prayer that ignites when the self-emptying of God meets the self-emptying aspiration of the creature:

I think that, if one were to come to an exact understanding, it would prove a blasphemy if anyone among created things were able to say that spiritual prayer can be prayed at all. For all prayer that can be prayed lies on this side of the spiritual realm. And all that is spiritual is a class that is free from movement and from prayer.[112]

As soon as the mind has crossed this boundary of pure prayer and proceeded inwards, it possesses neither prayer, nor emotions, nor tears, nor authority, nor freedom, nor petitions, nor desire, nor longing after any of those things which are hoped for in this world or in the world to come.

Therefore after pure prayer there is no longer prayer; all prayer's movements and forms, by the authority of their free will, conduct the mind thus far: for this reason struggle is involved; but beyond this limit there is wonder and no prayer. From here onwards the mind has ceased from prayer; there is sight, but the mind does not actively pray.[113]

As Clément says, we are 'offering the world on the altar of [our hearts]':

The condition of space–time which gives rise to the beating of the heart is no longer an endless prison, but a temple walled with light. The man 'feels' (taking the apophatic meaning of the 'feeling of God') the risen Christ, who is the face of the Father, in the light of the spirit.[114]

Only when the last element of creation has become transfigured through the tears of Christ living in us will tears cease. We do not pray, we are prayed.

We must remember that these are not tears of sorrow only, but both sorrow and joy. As Isaac says, 'Here is sweet and flaming compunction', or, to use the image of John Climacus, mixed like honey and the comb—mixed because in this singularity we somehow come to know more and more (in the most intimate biblical sense) that we gaze upon the face of God (Matthew 18:10–11). The promises made for us in baptism are fulfilled in us by this new and unceasing pouring out of fiery tears through our life within the blessed Trinity, whose love has become the polarity in this unending exchange of *kenosis*. This is the baptism of tears. The dark glass of experience through which we see is washed by tears that magnify the face of God as we behold. And the only sin of which we need repent is turning away from this beholding.

We come to know that in this singularity we are brought to the freedom and possibility of the primordial moment of creation. We know that water and fire are one, that our tears ignite God's fire upon the earth. Syriac literature and liturgies are full of this knowledge:

See, Fire and Spirit in the womb that bore you!
See, Fire and Spirit in the river where you were baptised!
Fire and Spirit in our Baptism;
In the Bread and in the Cup, Fire and Holy Spirit![115]

Tears break open our stony hearts; they become alabaster boxes from which the oil of the Spirit's anointing is poured upon the earth. We begin to understand that our tears, like the water Elijah poured out on the altar, ignite the baptism of fire which Christ has promised, salting creation with fire; his apophatic fire breaks out from all things.

As we pass through the strait place, we not only are drawn, we become impelled by the gaze of Love into infinite possibility of transfiguration. We become so found in God that self-reflection becomes less necessary and less possible. Our only security is the insecurity of listening unknowing, and then acting in faith on what is heard and given. Our prayer is being prayed. Our only perception is non-experience. Our longing no longer seeks fulfilment; indeed, it is no longer noticed as longing.

In the end, the way of tears and fire is a commitment not to have any way; not to have any way, that is, except God's way, that remains unknown until it is unfolded in the silence of mingled divine and human *kenosis*. In the words of Isaac of Nineveh:

From stillness a man can gain possession of the three (causes of tears): love of God, awestruck wonder at his mysteries, and humility of heart. Without these it is unthinkable that a man should be accounted worthy to taste of the wellspring of flaming compunction arising from the love of God. There is no passion so fervent as the love of God. O Lord, deem me worthy of this wellspring![116]

*

NOTES

1   Tr. Sebastian Brock, 'John the Solitary, *On Prayer*', *Journal of Theological Studies*, New Series, 30 (1979), p. 87.

2   Abraham of Nathpar, tr. Sebastian Brock, *The Syriac Fathers on Prayer and the Spiritual Life* (Cistercian, 1987), p. 195.

3   The passage uses *idou* (behold) three times. The New Jerusalem Bible translates all the occurrences with the analytical word 'look', and substitutes 'among' for 'within'. Jerome emphasises the interpretation I have given by translating the third *idou* in the Vulgate as *Amen!* instead of *ecce*. Isaac of Nineveh, drawing on a much earlier Syriac tradition, agrees explicitly that the kingdom of heaven has always meant contemplation. The filters of scholasticism, Calvinism, neo-scholasticism and positivism have eliminated the contemplative strands present in Hebrew and Greek from modern translations of the Bible and, consequently, often from the late-antique and medieval texts that rely on them.

4   Irenaeus, *Adversus Haereses* (*Against Heresies*), 4. 34. 5–7.

5   A meditation on Exodus 34:29–35 and Revelation 22:1–5.

6   Denali, 'The Great One' in Athabascan (formerly Mount McKinley). Along with Mount St Elias to the south-east, it is the highest geographical profile on earth, rising from a 3000-foot elevation plateau to 20,320 feet.

7   One might say that love is the weight of glory (*kavod*) that bestows substance.

8   Augustine, *Confessions* X.27.

9   See Gordon Lathrop, *Holy Ground: A Liturgical Cosmology* (Fortress Press, 2003).

10 I am grateful to the late C.A. Conway for some historical observations.

11 Today we equate rhetoric with 'spin'. But in the world of the Bible and in the medieval world, rhetoric was the means by which you established your relationship to the truth, both for yourself and in your interaction with the community. This task of learning rhetoric was moral and ethical, and pertained especially to the care with which you constructed your memory, so that what came out of your mouth would be both truthful and pertinent to the situation being addressed. (The notion of memory was not confined to the ability to memorise but involved the whole person: intuition, emotion, sensibility.) The care with which you thought and spoke determined how others judged your character. This was, at least theoretically, the foundation of politics. See the books on memory by Mary Carruthers, especially *The Craft of Thought: Meditation, Rhetoric and the Making of Images, 400–1200*, CUP, 1998. Religion is political in the best sense of ancient rhetoric; and the Bible, especially the New Testament, can be understood as a collection of rhetorical documents

by authors who have discerned the truth and write 'so that [we] may believe'. In other words, the Bible gives us difficult material in a form digestible to our memories and on which we can extemporise in an inventive and relevant way in any given situation. See Carruthers, *The Craft of Thought*, pp. 1–9 especially. This was, of course, the method of the rabbis at the time of Jesus, whose interpretations were specific as to person, context and situation. Hence all the jokes about ten rabbis and 15 opinions. Jesus himself used this method (see John 21:21–22).

12 Ursula K. Le Guin, *The Farthest Shore* (Bantam, 1969), p. 67.

13 *Nicomachean Ethics*, 10. We might think of this space as the centre of the Christian paradox (the 'therefore', *dio*, in Philippians 2:5–11) where resurrection is found. See 'The space of prayer', which follows, and my *Pillars of Flame: Power, Priesthood and Spiritual Maturity*, reissued by Seabury Press, 2007.

14 The term for primate in the Episcopal Church is 'Presiding Bishop'.

15 The full address, as well as the reflections that preceded it, can be found at the Archbishop of Canterbury's website: www.archbishopofcanterbury.org.

16 Benedicta Ward SLG, *Harlots of the Desert* (Mowbray, 1987).

17 *The Assessment of Inward Stirrings* [original Middle English title: *A Pistle of Discrecioun of Stirings*] in *The Pursuit of Wisdom*, trans. and ed. James A. Walsh SJ (Paulist Press, 1988), p. 137.

18 The *Cloud* author makes clear that 'the devil' is shorthand for 'the spirit of the flesh and the spirit of the world', which arises from the human heart. *The Discernment of Spirits* [original Middle English title: *A Tretis of Discrescyon of Spirites*], in Walsh, *The Pursuit of Wisdom*, p. 110.

19 Walsh, *The Pursuit of Wisdom*, p. 111.

20 *A Letter of Private Direction* [Middle English title: *The Book of Privy Counselling*] in Walsh, *The Pursuit of Wisdom*, p. 234.

21 *Assessment of Inward Stirrings*, pp. 141–142. It should be noted here that 'love' refers to the faculty of knowing God. See *The Cloud of Unknowing*, particularly chapters 4 and 6.

22 See especially Keith Thomas, *Religion and the Decline of Magic* (Charles Scriber's Sons, 1971) and Michael Camille, *The Gothic Idol* (CUP, 1987).

23 Chögyam Trumgpa, *Cutting Through Spiritual Materialism* (Shambhala, 1987).

24 Hilarion Alfeyev, *The Spiritual World of Isaac the Syrian* (Cistercian, 2000), p. 160.

25 *Religion and the Decline of Magic*, p. 61. He goes on to point out that attempts to reform idolatrous attitudes tend to push people into rituals on the one hand and ideology on the other.

26 Impasse is a different problem altogether. See Constance Fitzgerald's 'Impasse and dark night': www.geocities.com/baltimorecarmel/johncross/impasse.html.

27 *The Spiritual World of Isaac the Syrian*, pp. 162–163.

28 Maggie Ross, *The Fountain and the Furnace: The Way of Tears and Fire* (Paulist Press, 1987), pp. 230–31.

29 See my *Pillars of Flame* cited above.

30 Tr. Sebastian Brock in *The Fountain and the Furnace*, p. 251. The context may be found in *The Ascetical Homilies of Isaac the Syrian*, trans. Dana Miller (Holy Transfiguration Monastery, 1984), pp. 115–116; A.J. Wensinck, tr., *Mystic Treatises of Isaac of Nineveh*, Nieuwe Reeks, Deel XXIII, No. 1 (Wiesbaden, 1969), pp. 164–166.

31 Buddhists facilitate this sort of prayer by the practice of *tonglen*, breathing in darkness and breathing out light. See *The Tibetan Book of Living and Dying*, by Sogyal Rinpoche (HarperSanFrancisco, 1993).

32 Hymn on Faith 10:17, quoted in Sebastian Brock, *The Luminous Eye: The Spiritual World Vision of St Ephrem the Syrian* (Cistercian, 1992), p. 94.

33 For this story see www.cnn.com/2007/TECH/science/12/24/ice.walrus.ap/index.html

34 For more on Nature Deficit Disorder, see Bradford McKee, 'Growing Up Denatured', *New York Times* (April 28, 2005).

35 See Charles Siebert, 'Planet of the Retired Apes', *New York Times* (July 24, 2005) (online edition).

36 Irenaeus '… is the first writer to have a Christian Bible before him… [He] completed the first great synthesis of Christian thought… what became the main elements of Christian doctrine' (Eric Osborn, *Irenaeus of Lyons*, CUP, 2001, pp. xi, xiv, 10).

37 On the work of silence, see 'Practical adoration' following.

38 www.archbishopofcanterbury.org/1372.

39 From ancient times it has been considered blasphemous to pronounce the name of God, whether YHWH or I AM.

40 www.archbishopofcanterbury.org/1374

41 www.archbishopofcanterbury.org/2857

42 The Book of Common Prayer (The Church Hymnal Corporation, 1977), p. 336. See Romans 12:1.

43 Julian of Norwich, Long Text, Chapter 19: '… the inward drawith the outeward by grace, and bothe shal be onyd in blisse without end by the vertue of Christe.' Note to the reader: there is no adequate translation of Julian's text, but reading the Middle English of the Glasscoe edition is no more difficult than reading a text message and uses the same skills. See *Julian of Norwich: A Revelation of Love*, ed. Marion Glasscoe, 2nd rev. ed. (University of Exeter Press, 1993).

44 *Julian of Norwich: A Revelation of Love*, ch. 13: 'Also I saw our lord scorne his [the devil's] malice and nowten his onmigte, and he wil that we doe so'. ['Scorn' in Middle English means 'ignore' as well.]

45 See the discussion in 'Cranberries' above.

46 'You speak in my heart and say, "Seek my face." Your face, Lord, will I seek' (Psalm 17:11, BCP 1972).

47 Bernard of Clairvaux insisted that the ascension was the most important event in the Gospels and in the life of Christ. See Bernard McGinn, *The Growth of Mysticism: From Gregory the Great to the Twelfth Century* (SCM, 1994), p. 176. See also V. Gillespie and M. Ross, 'The Apophatic Image: The Poetics of Effacement in Julian of Norwich' in *The Medieval Mystical Tradition in England V*, ed. M. Glasscoe (D.S. Brewer, 1992), pp. 53–77.

48 Composite translation.

49 We might understand 1 Corinthians 13:12 in this way: through our experience we see as in a mirror darkly, but beholding we see face to face.

50 Ephrem the Syrian, *Hymns on Faith* 14:5 in *The Luminous Eye*.

51 See Fraser Watts and Mark Williams, *The Psychology of Religious Knowing* (CUP, 1988).

52 See Zephaniah 1:7, 12–18. The author talks about consequence using the prophetic (and possibly ironic) rhetorical strategy of assigning the first person to God, but it is clear that he understands that it is not a vengeful God that will bring about disaster, but the folly of the complacent. Out of that desolation the tenderness of God will bring us home (3:20).

53 Holy Week seems to be fertile ground for liturgical aberrations. One of the worst I ever saw was at noon on Good Friday. A huge wooden cross was laid on the altar steps. Two women deacons in white albs snuggled into the spaces on either side between the upright and the crosspiece. Then they proceeded to anoint the cross with oil and stick rose petals all over it while Celtic harps tinkled in the background.

54 Diarmaid MacCulloch, *Christianity: The First Three Thousand Years* (Viking, 2010).

55 O. Clément, 'Purification by Atheism', in *Orthodoxy and the Death of God: Essays in Contemporary Theology*, ed. A.M. Allchin. Studies supplementary to *Sobornost*, Vol. I (Fellowship of St Alan and St Sergius, 1971).

56 Reproductions of these icons may be found in *Byzantium: Faith and Power (1261–1557)*, ed. Helen C. Evans (The Metropolitan Museum of Art, 2004), p. 126. Unfortunately, the faces on the fish do not show up in the photograph. Not every item in the exhibit is in this catalogue. Many of the items from St Catherine's Monastery are in a companion volume, *Saint Catherine's Monastery, Sinai, Egypt: A Photographic Essay*, text by Helen C. Evans, photographs by Bruce White, The Metropolitan Museum of Art in collaboration with Saint Catherine's Monastery, Sinai, 2004.

57 Evans, *Saint Catherine's Monastery*, p. 76.

58 A liturgical garment in the form of a knee-length tunic worn primarily by deacons and occasionally by bishops.

59 Evans, *Byzantium*, pp. 302–303.

60 Evans, *Saint Catherine's Monastery*, p. 70.

61 Evans, *Byzantium*, p. 278.

62 Evans, *Byzantium*, pp. 95 ff.

63 Evans, *Saint Catherine's Monastery*, p. 64.

64 Peter Schjeldahl, 'Striking God', *The New Yorker* (May 17, 2004), p. 101.

65 Jean-Honoré Fragonard (1732–1806) is considered one of the major figures of the rococo style in 18th-century French painting. Fragonard is best known for sensuous works depicting the carefree amusements of the French aristocracy.

66 A name for Mary, 'the God-bearing'.

67 A large cloth embroidered with a near life-sized icon of Christ in the Tomb, used for veneration on Good Friday.

68 Evans, *Byzantium*, p. vii.

69 Andrew Anthony, 'Risky Business', *The Observer* (August 1, 2004). See also Umberto Eco's hilarious essay, tr. William Weaver, *Travels in Hyperreality* (HBJ, 1973), pp. 22–58.

70 See Kallistos Ware, *The Orthodox Way* (St Vladimir's Seminary Press, 1980), p. 98.

71 Ware, *The Orthodox Way*, p. 146.

72 Fra Angelico is an exception, as can be seen by comparing his paintings intended for public viewing and those in the cells of San Marco. See, for example, Christopher Lloyd, *Fra Angelico* (Phaidon Press, 1991).

73 This is one of the most important distinctions in the Bible that is often obscured in translation.

74 The phrase is Belden Lane's, *The Solace of Fierce Landscapes: Exploring Desert and Mountain Spirituality* (OUP, 1998).

75 Martin Andic, 'Simone Weil and Plotinus', unpublished paper, emphasis in the original.

76 *The Sayings of the Desert Fathers*, trans. Benedicta Ward SLG (Cistercian, 1975), p. 118. Abba Moses, 6.

77 Tr. Sebastian Brock. Also see Alfeyev, *The Spiritual World of Isaac the Syrian*, p. 120.

78 Tr. Sebastian Brock. Also see Alfeyev, *The Spiritual World of Isaac the Syrian*, p. 112.

79 This article was originally dedicated to the memory of the Reverend Professor Charles Abbott Conway † 26 August 2007.

80 Alfeyev, *The Spiritual World of Isaac the Syrian*, pp. 219–20. Isaac is quoting another Syrian monk, Pseudo-Dionysius.

Notes

81 Alfeyev, *The Spiritual World of Isaac the Syrian*, p. 252.

82 Anyone who prays is aware of this process, but until Martin Laird invented the term *logophasis*, there had been no way to speak of it simply. See his *Gregory of Nyssa and the Grasp of Faith: Union, Knowledge, and Divine Presence* (OUP, 2004), and the discussion below.

83 Laird, *Gregory of Nyssa and the Grasp of Faith*, p. 32.

84 Alfeyev, *The Spiritual World of Isaac the Syrian*, p. 159

85 Alfeyev, *The Spiritual World of Isaac the Syrian*, p. 267.

86 *The Paradox of Intention: Reaching the Goal by Giving Up the Attempt to Reach It*, American Academy of Religion Studies in Religion, no. 48 (Scholars Press, 1988).

87 For an illuminating discussion of experience vs beholding, see *I and Thou* by Martin Buber, tr. Walter Kaufmann (T&T Clark, 1979).

88 What is being remembered/interpreted, perhaps, is the threshold, the tipping point at which our self-consciousness disappears. For a visual interpretation of this process in a late-13th-century manuscript, do an internet search for Rothschild Canticles and click on the Flickr link.

89 See 'Tears and fire' in this volume.

90 The Greek is *kosmos* and can mean any system, but in the Gospel of John one of the main themes is that Jesus is the new temple, as, by virtue of being co-heirs, each of us is as well. This interpretation accords with his other speeches about the temple.

91 Georges Duby and Philippe Braunstein, 'The Emergence of the Individual' in *A History of Private Life*, vol. II, *Revelations of the Medieval World*, ed. Georges Duby, trans. Arthur Goldhammer (Belknap Press, 1988), p. 619.

92 Alfeyev, *The Spiritual World of Isaac the Syrian*, p. 192.

93 Alfeyev, *The Spiritual World of Isaac the Syrian*, pp. 211–212.

94 This insight into John's use of the *pistis*-words for 'faith' is from an unpublished paper by Judith Lieu, given at the Oxford Classics Seminar on Faith in the Ancient World, Autumn, 2006, Oxford. Paul promotes the same idea using the word 'hope' in Romans 8:24–25.

95 See 'Tears and fire' following.

96 See, for example, Joan Breton Connelly, *Portrait of a Priestess: Women and Ritual in Ancient Greece* (Princeton University Press, 2007).

97 See The New English Hymnal, 244.

98 Tr. Sebastian Brock, in *The Fountain and the Furnace*, p. 185.

99 Tr. Sebastian Brock, *The Harp of the Spirit*, Issue 4 of *Studies Supplementary to Sobornost* (Borgo Press, 1983), pp. 62–63.

100 Tr. Sebastian Brock in *The Fountain and the Furnace*, pp. 85–85. See also Miller, *The Ascetical Homilies of Isaac the Syrian*, p. 15; and Wensinck, *Mystic Treatises*

of Isaac of Nineveh, p. 13. It should be noted that the page numbers cited in Wensinck are those of the original in the margin of the translation.

101 From a sermon first preached at Christ Church, Oxford, and later published as 'Holy Space' in *Open to Judgement: Sermons and Addresses*, Rowan Williams (DLT, 1994), p. 101; the reference to Westcott is in Williams' *On Christian Theology* (Wiley-Blackwell, 1999), p. 186, note 11.

102 Tr. Sebastian Brock; Miller, *Ascetical Homilies*, p. 312; Wensinck, *Mystical Treatises*, p. 455.

103 'Isaac of Antioch', tr. Sebastian Brock, in *Syriac Perspectives on Late Antiquity* (Variorum, 1984), pp. v, 27–28.

104 See Gerald May, *Will and Spirit: A Contemplative Psychology* (HarperSanFrancisco, 1982).

105 Tr. Sebastian Brock in *The Fountain and the Furnace*, p. 189; Miller, *Ascetical Homilies*, p. 174; Wensinck, *Mystical Treatises*, p. 245.

106 Tr. Sebastian Brock in *Pillars of Flame*, p. 125.

107 Both paragraphs tr. Sebastian Brock, quoted in *The Fountain and the Furnace*, p. 165; Miller, *Ascetical Homilies*, p. 345; Wensinck, *Mystical Treatises*, pp. 507–508; Miller, *Ascetical Homilies*, p. 383; Wensinck, *Mystical Treatises*, p. 577.

108 Tr. Sebastian Brock in *The Fountain and the Furnace*, pp. 185–186; Miller, *Ascetical Homilies*, pp. 82–83. Wensinck, *Mystical Treatises*, p. 86.

109 Olivier Clément, 'Purification by Atheism', *Orthodoxy and the Death of God*, ed. A.M. Allchin, *Supplements to Sobornost 1*, 1971, pp. 31–32.

110 Olivier Clément, 'The Holy Spirit and Monasticism Today', *Cistercian Studies* xiv 4, p. 321.

111 Tr. Sebastian Brock in 'Isaac of Nineveh: Some Newly Discovered Works', *Sobornost/ECR* 8:1, 1986, p. 2.

112 Tr. Sebastian Brock in *The Fountain and the Furnace*, p. 253; Miller, *Ascetical Homilies*, p. 118; Wensinck, *Mystical Treatises*, p. 168.

113 Tr. Sebastian Brock, *The Fountain and the Furnace*, p. 251.

114 Olivier Clément, 'The Holy Spirit in Monasticism Today', p. 323.

115 'A Hymn of St Ephrem to Christ on the Incarnation, the Holy Spirit and the Sacrament' tr. Robert Murray, *ECR* 3 (1970), pp. 142–150.

116 Unpublished translation by Dana Miller, Isaac of Nineveh, Book II.